READING MACHINES

TOPICS IN THE DIGITAL HUMANITIES

Humanities computing is redefining basic principles about research and publication. An influx of new, vibrant, and diverse communities of practitioners recognizes that computer applications are subject to continual innovation and reappraisal. This series publishes books that demonstrate the new questions, methods, and results arising in the digital humanities.

SERIES EDITORS

Susan Schreibman
Raymond C. Siemens

READING MACHINES

TOWARD AN ALGORITHMIC CRITICISM

STEPHEN RAMSAY

UNIVERSITY OF ILLINOIS PRESS

Urbana, Chicago, and Springfield

Library of Congress Cataloging-in-Publication Data
Ramsay, Stephen.
Reading machines : toward an algorithmic criticism /
Stephen Ramsay.
p. cm. — (Topics in the digital humanities)
Includes bibliographical references and index.
ISBN 978-0-252-03641-5 (cloth) —
ISBN 978-0-252-07820-0 (pbk.)
1. Linguistic String Parser (Computer grammar)
2. Discourse analysis—Data processing.
3. Reading machines (Data processing equipment)
I. Title.
P98.5.P38R36   2011
401'.41—dc22   2011006829

For William and Mary Ramsay

One no longer noticed the accidents of things but only the substance of the universe, and this is why we did not care whether the flawless surface was a liquid equilibrated according to eternal laws, or a diamond, impervious except under a light falling from above.

—Alfred Jarry, *Exploits and Opinions
of Dr. Faustroll, Pataphysician*

CONTENTS

PRECONDITIONS

When Willard McCarty proposed that we "ask in the context of computing what can (and must) be known of our artefacts, how we know what we know about them and how new knowledge is made," he undoubtedly meant to lift our gaze above the merely practical matters suggested by the term "humanities computing" (McCarty 1231). For to ask such questions "in the context of computing" is to suggest that computing belongs in the rarefied atmosphere of epistemology—that it is less a matter of doing (or allowing, or facilitating) this or that with the human record, and more a matter of providing an additional, and perhaps an uncommonly fertile, occasion for theoretical musing and contemplation. For McCarty, actual results are less important than the insights gained from the juxtaposition of mechanism and mind. The field can proudly and justly describe itself as "the quest for meaningful failure" (1232).

Against this view stand those who regard computers in the humanities as providing a welcome relief from the radical skepticism of contemporary humanistic thought. Here, after all, is a machine that not only gives answers but also demands them—a device that is wholly intolerant toward equivocation and uncertainty. In this view, the computer represents an emancipation from the ironic imprisonments of postmodern excess. Even without supposing that computation leads toward (or even begins with) objectivity, some see it as a way to get beyond the beached solipsism that characterizes modern *discours* and toward its right and proper end in *raison*. It is scientific method joined to humanistic inquiry. It is the dream of Descartes tempered by the dream of Leibniz.

Computers are perhaps chief among those tools we routinely describe as "changing everything," and yet neither of the desiderata stated above are particularly startling when offered as descriptions of that change. Both try to dilate the revolution in terms of what is already familiar to us: the former, by installing computation within the context of present theoretical concerns; the latter, by claiming it for the partisans of older, surer methods. One tries to kick away the ladder; the other holds to it more firmly than ever. Eloquent expressions are to be found on either side. If, amid all the excitement that presently surrounds computing in the humanities, one still hears the two most dreaded of all academic judgments—"Is that all?" and "What does this have to do with us?"—it is undoubtedly because we have mostly chosen to describe ourselves either in terms that are meant to comfort the larger and older disciplines from which this new community of practice was formed, or to suggest that ours is too radical a break to be contained by them. Like all revolutions, digital humanities derives some of its kinetic energy from swinging between these two poles.

This is a book about literary text analysis—a particular form of scholarly engagement within the much broader field of interests, concerns, and endeavors we now call digital humanities. But it is more fundamentally a book that tries to locate a hermeneutics at the boundary between mechanism and theory. The "algorithmic criticism" proposed here seeks, in the narrowing forces of constraint embodied and instantiated in the strictures of programming, an analogue to the liberating potentialities of art. It proposes that we create tools—practical, instrumental, verifiable mechanisms—that enable critical engagement, interpretation, conversation, and contemplation. It proposes that we channel the heightened objectivity made possible by the machine into the cultivation of those heightened subjectivities necessary for critical work.

The precise nature of scientific inquiry, well revised and reimagined in recent years by theorists and historians from a variety of disciplines, is well beyond the scope of this book. But for decades the dominant assumption within humanities computing—evident even in the most recent examples cited in these pages—has been that if the computer is to be useful to the humanist, its efficacy must necessarily lie in the aptness of the scientific metaphor for humanistic study. This work takes the contrary view and proposes that scientific method and metaphor (or, more precisely, the use of these notions within the distorted epistemology we call "scientism") is, for the most part, incompatible with the terms of humanistic endeavor. The dilation of algorithmic criticism begins, then, with a consideration of how that scientific method has been used and abused within humanities computing itself.

Envisioning an alternative to the strictures of the scientific metaphor entails reaching for other, more obviously humanistic models. Chapter 2 takes up this challenge by turning to the scientific imaginary as it appears in the realm of art. The variegated history of the *querelle* between art and science is, again, beyond the scope of the discussion offered here, but it will not be controversial to assert that art has very often sought either to parody science or to diminish its claims to truth. Within this important post-Romantic strain of critique, this work isolates another voice that has sought to find a common imaginative ground between art and science. The chapter begins with Alfred Jarry's inauguration of the "science of 'Pataphysics" and ends with the literary refraction of Jarry's *Gedankenexperimenten* in the work of the Oulipo. The latter, in which the terms of art and criticism are uniquely joined, informs algorithmic criticism's emphasis on the liberating forces of (computationally enforced) constraint. I argue, moreover, that this important modernist genealogy points to the primacy of pattern as the basic hermeneutical function that unites art, science, and criticism.

Chapter 3 takes up the literary critical analogues to the poetics of constraint. The notion of "deformance" provides the critical framework for a discussion of conventional criticism as an activity dependent upon the notions of constraint, procedure, and alternative formation. It is in this light that computationally enacted textual transformations reveal themselves most clearly as self-consciously extreme forms of those hermeneutical procedures found in all interpretative acts. Close analysis of several apparently diverse critical works—from readings of the *I Ching* and Saussure's anagrams to medieval poetry and Shakespearean sonnets—reveals the essential deformative nature of critical reading.

Programming, which algorithmic criticism reframes as the enactment of a critical reading strategy, undergirds all of these meditations. Chapter 4 delves deeper into the terms of this variety of textual activity, in an attempt to unite the reductive calculus of computation to the broader act of critical narrative. Using the Turing test as a guide, I attempt to locate the theoretical components that would allow computer-assisted criticism to be situated within the broader context of literary study. These considerations make way for chapter 5, which surveys some of the newer text-analytical tools—claiming them, unabashedly, as potential instruments of algorithmic criticism.

I have many people to thank for countless hours of conversation, inspiration, and insight—above all, Jerome McGann, Johanna Drucker, Willard McCarty, Martin Mueller, Mark Olsen, Geoffrey Rockwell, Stan Ruecker, Stéfan Sinclair, and John Unsworth, all of whom read drafts of these pages and whose conversation enlightened the path. Being in the company of these thoughtful and learned scholars did more than anything to bring this project to fruition. They will find their ideas deformed on every page.

Many thanks are also due to the members of the research groups with which I've been associated over the years, including the University of Virginia's Institute for Advanced Technology in the Humanities, Virginia Center for Digital History, and Speculative Computing Lab; the Ivanhoe Working Group; the Text Analysis Developers Alliance; the University of Nebraska–Lincoln's Center for Digital Research in the Humanities; and the MONK Project. I am deeply honored to have been a part of these extraordinary centers of activity. The dozens of scholars, engineers, digital humanists, media theorists, and administrators I alias with this list have made the task of writing a book about the future they represent a pleasurable one. I am especially proud to have worked with Tanya Clement, Matt Kirschenbaum, Worthy Martin, Bethanie Nowviskie, Daniel Pitti, Ken Price, Brian Pytlik-Zillig, Sara Steger, Will Thomas, Kay Walter; my intrepid editors at the University of Illinois Press, Ray Siemens, Bill Regier, Susan Schreibman; and my copyeditor, Jill Hughes.

I owe an enormous debt of thanks to my wife, June, who read this work to the point of memorization and suggested improvements with gentleness and care. My parents—to whom this work is lovingly dedicated—offered me a gift that in subtle ways informs this work at its core: never once did they ask me what I was going to do with it.

1 AN ALGORITHMIC CRITICISM

Digital humanities, like most fields of scholarly inquiry, constituted itself through a long accretion of revolutionary insight, territorial rivalry, paradigmatic rupture, and social convergence. But the field is unusual in that it has often pointed both to a founder and to a moment of creation. The founder is Roberto Busa, an Italian Jesuit priest who in the late 1940s undertook the production of an automatically generated concordance to the works of Thomas Aquinas using a computer. The founding moment was the creation of a radically transformed, reordered, disassembled, and reassembled version of one of the world's most influential philosophies:

00596 in veniale peccatum non cadat; ut sic hoc verbum habemus non determinatum, sed confusum praesens importet
-003(3SN)3.3.2.b.ex/56

00597 intellegit profectum scientiae christi quantum ad experientiam secundum novam conversionem ad sensibile praesens,
-S 003(3SN)14.1.3e.ra4/4

00598 ita quot apprehenditur ut possibile adipisce, aprehenditur ut jam quodammodo praesens: et ideo spec delectationem
-003(3SN)26.1.2.ra3/8

00599 operationibus: quia illud quod certudinaliter quasi praesens tenemus per intellectum, dicimur sentire, vel videre;
-003(3Sn)26.1.5.co/11 (*Index* 65129)

Undertaking such transformations for the purpose of humanistic inquiry would eventually come to be called "text analysis," and in literary study, computational text analysis has been used to study problems related to style and authorship for nearly sixty years. As the field has matured, it has incorporated elements of some of the most advanced forms of technical endeavor, including natural language processing, statistical computing, corpus linguistics, data mining, and artificial intelligence. It is easily the most quantitative approach to the study of literature, arguably the oldest form of digital literary study, and, in the opinion of many, the most scientific form of literary investigation.

But "algorithmic criticism"—*criticism* derived from algorithmic manipulation of text—either does not exist or exists only in nascent form. The digital revolution, for all its wonders, has not penetrated the core activity of literary studies, which, despite numerous revolutions of a more epistemological nature, remains mostly concerned with the interpretative analysis of written cultural artifacts. Texts are browsed, searched, and disseminated by all but the most hardened Luddites in literary study, but seldom are they transformed algorithmically as a means of gaining entry to the deliberately and self-consciously subjective act of critical interpretation. Even text analysis practitioners avoid bringing the hermeneutical freedom of criticism to the "outputted" text. Bold statements, strong readings, and broad generalizations (to say nothing of radical misreadings, anarchic accusations, and agonistic paratextual revolts) are rare, if not entirely absent from the literature of the field, where the emphasis is far more often placed on methodology and the limitations it imposes.

It is perhaps not surprising that text analysis would begin this way. Busa's own revolution was firmly rooted in the philological traditions to which modern criticism was largely a reaction. Reflecting on the creation of the *Index* some forty years after the fact, Busa offered the following motivations:

> I realized first that a philological and lexicographical inquiry into the verbal system of an author has to precede and prepare for a doctrinal interpretation of his works. Each writer expresses his conceptual system in and through his verbal system, with the consequence that the reader who masters this verbal system, using his own conceptual system, has to get an insight into the writer's conceptual system. The reader should not simply attach to the words he reads the significance they have in his mind, but should try to find out what significance they had in the author's mind. ("Annals" 83)

Such ideas would not have seemed unusual to nineteenth-century biblical scholars, for whom meaning was something both knowable and recoverable through careful, scientific analysis of language, genre, textual recension, and historical context. Nor would it, with some rephrasing, have been a radical proposition either for Thomas himself or for the Dominican friars who produced the first concordance (to the Vulgate) in the thirteenth century. However, we do no injustice to Busa's achievement in noting that the contemporary critical ethos regards Busa's central methodological tenets as grossly naive. Modern criticism, increasingly skeptical of authorial intention as a normative principle and linguistic meaning as a stable entity, has largely abandoned the idea that we could ever keep from reading ourselves into the reading of an author and is no longer concerned with attempting to avoid this conundrum.

But even in Busa's highly conventional methodological project, with its atomized fragmentation of a divine text, we can discern the enormous liberating power of the computer. In the original formation of Thomas's text, "presence" was a vague leitmotif. But on page 65,129 of the algorithmically transformed text, "presence" is that toward which every formation tends, the central feature of every utterance, and the pattern that orders all that surrounds it. We encounter "ut sic hoc" and "ut possibile," but the transformed text does not permit us to complete those thoughts. Even Busa would have had to concede that the effect is not the immediate apprehension of knowledge, but instead what the Russian Formalists called *ostranenie*—the estrangement and defamiliarization of textuality. One might suppose that being able to see texts in such strange and unfamiliar ways would give such procedures an important place in the critical revolution the Russian Formalists ignited—which is to say, the movement that ultimately gave rise to the hermeneutical philosophies that would supplant Busa's own methodology.

But text analysis would take a much more conservative path. Again and again in the literature of text analysis, we see a movement back toward the hermeneutics of Busa, with the analogy of science being put forth as the highest aspiration of digital literary study. For Roseanne Potter, writing in the late 1980s, "the principled use of technology and criticism" necessarily entailed criticism becoming "absolutely comfortable with scientific methods" (91–92). Her hope, shared by many in the field, was that the crossover might create a criticism "suffused with humanistic values," but there was never a suggestion that the "scientific methods" of algorithmic manipulation might need to establish comfort with the humanities. After all, it was the humanities that required deliverance from the bitter malady that had overtaken modern criticism: "In our own day, professors of literature indulge in what John Ellis (1974) somewhat mockingly called 'wise eclecticism'—a general tendency to believe that if you can compose an interesting argument to support a position, any well-argued assertion is as valid as the next one. A scientific literary criticism would not permit some of the most widespread of literary critical practices" (93). Those not openly engaged in the hermeneutics of "anything goes"—historicists old or new—were presented with the settling logic of truth and falsehood proposed by computational analysis:

This is not to deny the historical, social, and cultural context of literature (Bakhtin, 1981), and of language itself (Halliday, 1978). Nor can one overlook the very rich and subtle elaborations of literary theory in the forty years since Barthes published *Le degré zéro de l'écriture* (1953). In point of fact, most of these elaborations have the technical status of hypothesis, since they have not been confirmed empirically in terms of the data which they propose to describe—literary texts. This is where computer techniques and computer data come into their own. (Fortier 376)

Susan Hockey, in a book intended not only to survey the field of humanities computing but also to "explain the intellectual rationale for electronic text technology in the humanities," later offered a vision of the role of the computer in literary study to which most contemporary text analysis practitioners fully subscribe:

> Computers can assist with the study of literature in a variety of ways, some more successful than others. . . . Computer-based tools are especially good for comparative work, and here some simple statistical tools can help to reinforce the interpretation of the material. These studies are particularly suitable for testing hypotheses or for verifying intuition. They can provide concrete evidence to support or refute hypotheses or interpretations which have in the past been based on human reading and the somewhat serendipitous noting of interesting features. (66)

It is not difficult to see why a contemporary criticism temperamentally and philosophically at peace with intuition and serendipity would choose to ignore the corrective tendencies of the computer against the deficiencies of "human reading." Text analysis arises to assist the critic, but only if the critic agrees to operate within the regime of scientific methodology with its "refutations" of hypotheses.

Perhaps the boldest expression of these ideas comes from a 2008 editorial in the *Boston Globe* titled "Measure for Measure." In it, literary critic Jonathan Gottschall describes the field of literary studies itself as "moribund, aimless, and increasingly irrelevant to the concerns not only of the 'outside world,' but also to the world inside the ivory tower." The solution is one that even C. P. Snow would have found provocative:

> I think there is a clear solution to this problem. Literary studies should become more like the sciences. Literature professors should apply science's research methods, its theories, its statistical tools, and its insistence on hypothesis and proof. Instead of philosophical despair about the possibility of knowledge, they should embrace science's spirit of intellectual optimism. If they do, liter-

ary studies can be transformed into a discipline in which real understanding of literature and the human experience builds up along with all of the words.

This proposal may distress many of my colleagues, who may worry that adopting scientific methods would reduce literary study to a branch of the sciences. But if we are wise, we can admit that the sciences are doing many things better than we are, and gain from studying their successes, without abandoning the things that make literature special.

Gottschall offers no suggestions for how we might retain those things that make humanistic discourse itself "special." He admits to being not overly fond of what he presumes to be the main outlines of that discourse (the "beauty myth," the death of the author, the primacy of social and cultural influences in the constitution of identity, and the sexism of the Western canon), but his main concern is that such notions have become the unexamined ground truths of contemporary criticism. This in itself is hardly objectionable; it is difficult to imagine a healthy episteme that does not constantly question even its most cherished assumptions. But that these ideas were themselves the product of decades of humanistic reflection and debate, that they supplanted other ideas that had come to be regarded as similarly uncontroversial, and that they provide a powerful counterexample to the "philosophical despair about the possibility of knowledge" against which he inveighs seems not to lessen Gottschall's faith in final answers. Only the methodologies of science and the rigor of computation can render unexamined assumptions "falsifiable."

Even Franco Moretti, whose outlook on literary study is assuredly quite different from Gottschall's, shows strong evidence of embracing this faith in the falsifiable: "I began this chapter by saying that quantitative data are useful because they are independent of interpretation; then, that they are challenging because they often demand an interpretation that transcends the quantitative realm; now, most radically, we see them *falsify* existing theoretical explanations, and ask for a theory, not so much of 'the' novel, but of *a whole family of novelistic forms*. A theory—of diversity" (*Graphs* 30). Moretti is right to be excited about what he is doing. It is breathtaking to see his graphs, maps, and trees challenging accepted notions about the nineteenth-century novel. But one wonders why it is necessary to speak of these insights as proceeding from that which is "independent of interpretation" and which leads to the "falsification" of ideas obtained through more conventional humanistic means. It is as if everything under discussion is a rhetorical object *except* the "data." The data is presented to us—in all of these cases—not as something that is also in need of interpretation, but as Dr. Johnson's stone hurtling through the space of our limited vision.

The procedure that Busa used to transform Thomas into an alternative text is, like most text-analytical procedures, algorithmic in the strictest sense. If science has repeatedly suggested itself as the most appropriate metaphor, it is undoubtedly because such algorithms are embedded in activities that appear to have the character of experiment. Busa, in the first instance, had formed an hypothesis concerning the importance of certain concepts in the work. He then sought to determine the parameters (in the form of suitable definitions and abstractions) for an experiment that could adjudicate the viability of this hypothesis. The experiment moved through the target environment (the text) with the inexorability of a scientific instrument creating observable effects at every turn. The observations were then used to confirm the hypothesis with which he began.

Some literary-critical problems clearly find comfort within such a framework. Authorship attribution, for example, seeks definitive answers to empirical questions concerning whether or not a work is by a particular author. Programs designed to adjudicate such questions can often be organized scientifically with hypotheses, control groups, validation routines, and reproducible methods. The same is true for any text analysis procedure that endeavors to expose the bare empirical facts of a text (often a necessary prelude to textual criticism and analytical bibliography). Hermeneutically, such investigations rely upon a variety of philosophical positivism in which the accumulation of verified, falsifiable facts forms the basis for interpretative judgment. In these particular discursive fields, the veracity of statements like "The tenth letter of *The Federalist* was written by James Madison" or "The 1597 quarto edition of *Romeo and Juliet* is a memorial reconstruction" are understood to hinge more or less entirely on the support of concrete textual evidence. One might challenge the interpretation of the facts, or even the factual nature of the evidence, but from a rhetorical standpoint, facts are what permit or deny judgment.

For most forms of critical endeavor, however, appeals to "the facts" prove far less useful. Consider, for example, Miriam Wallace's discussion of subjectivity in Virginia Woolf's novel *The Waves:*

> In this essay I want to resituate *The Waves* as complexly formulating and reformulating subjectivity through its playful formal style and elision of corporeal materiality. *The Waves* models an alternative subjectivity that exceeds the dominant (white, male, heterosexual) individual western subject through its stylistic usage of metaphor and metonymy. . . . Focusing on the narrative construction of subjectivity reveals the pertinence of *The Waves* for current feminist reconfigurations of the feminine subject. This focus links the novel's visionary limitations to the historic moment of Modernism. (295–96)

Wallace frames her discourse as a "resituation" of Woolf's novel within several larger fields of critical discourse. This will presumably involve the marshaling of evidence and the annunciation of claims. It may even involve offering various "facts" in support of her conclusions. But hermeneutically, literary critical arguments of this sort do not stand in the same relationship to facts, claims, and evidence as the more empirical forms of inquiry. There is no experiment that can verify the idea that Woolf's "playful formal style" reformulates subjectivity or that her "elision of corporeal materiality" exceeds the dominant Western subject. There is no control group that can contain "current feminist reconfigurations." And surely there is no metric by which we may quantify "pertinence" either for Woolf or for the author's own judgment.

The hermeneutical implications of these absences invoke ancient suspicions toward rhetoric, and in particular, toward the rhetorical office of *inventio:* the sophistic process of seeking truth through the dialectical interplay of trust, emotion, logic, and tradition, which has, since the seventeenth century, contended with the promises of empiricism (Bold 543–44). In some sense, humanistic discourse seems to lack methodology; it cannot describe the ground rules of engagement, the precise means of verification, or even the parameters of its subject matter. Yet as Gadamer pointed out in *Truth and Method:*

> The hermeneutic phenomenon is basically not a problem of method at all. It is not concerned with a method of understanding by means of which texts are subjected to scientific investigation like all other objects of experience. It is not concerned primarily with amassing verified knowledge, such as would satisfy the methodological ideal of science—yet it too is concerned with knowledge and with truth. . . . But what kind of knowledge and what kind of truth? (544)

Gadamer's question is not easily answered, but we may say that from a purely cultural standpoint, literary criticism operates at a register in which understanding, knowledge, and truth occur outside of the narrower denotative realm in which scientific statements are made. It is not merely the case that literary criticism is concerned with something other than the amassing of verified knowledge. Literary criticism operates within a hermeneutical framework in which the specifically scientific meaning of fact, metric, verification, and evidence simply do not apply. The "facts" of Woolf—however we choose to construe this term—are not the principal objects of study in literary criticism, and "evidence" stands as a metaphor for the delicate building blocks of rhetorical persuasion. We "measure" only to establish webs of interrelation and influence. "Verification" occurs in a social community of scholars whose agreement or disagreement is almost never put forth without qualification.

All of this leaves the project of text analysis in a difficult position. For even if we are willing to concede the general utility of computational methods for the project of humanistic inquiry, we must nonetheless contend with a fundamental disjunction between literary-critical method and computational method. The logic that underlies computation, though not scientific in the strict sense of the term, conforms easily to the methodologies of science. Computers are, as Hockey noted, good at counting, measuring, and (in a limited sense) verifying data, and we judge the tractability of data by the degree to which it can serve the requirements of these procedures. When it comes to literary criticism, however, we find that the "data" is almost entirely intractable from the standpoint of the computational rubric. Paper-based textual artifacts must either be transformed from a continuous field into some more quantized form (i.e., digitized), or accompanied, as in the case of markup, with an elaborate scaffolding by which the vagaries of continuity can be flattened and consistently recorded. We accept the compromises inherent in such transformations in order to reap the benefits of speed, automation, and scale that computational representations afford. But the situation is considerably more complicated in the case of the analysis that is undertaken with these objects. Not a single statement in Wallace's précis, and indeed very few of the statements one encounters in literary critical discourse, can be treated in this way. No extant computer can draw the conclusions that Wallace does by analyzing the links between "the novel's visionary limitations" and "the historic moment of Modernism"—particularly since the Modernism being invoked here is not a matter of shifting consumer prices or birth statistics. Literary-critical interpretation is not just a qualitative matter; it is also an insistently subjective manner of engagement.

Given the essential properties of computation, we might conclude that text analysis is precisely designed to frame literary-critical problems in terms of something analogous to consumer prices and birth statistics, and in general text analysis has chosen low-level linguistic phenomena as its primary object of study. Doing so would seem to demand that we assume the methodological posture of computational linguistics, with its (entirely appropriate) claims toward scientific rigor. According to this hermeneutical vision, text analysis is simply incapable of forming the sorts of conclusions that lie outside of a relatively narrow range of propositions.

It is not at all uncommon to encounter explicit statements of such interpretative limitation in text-analytical scholarship. John Burrows and D. H. Craig's use of principal component analysis for comparing Romantic and Renaissance tragedy—a masterful work of text-analytical scholarship by any measure—is typical in how it commits itself to an essentially scientific vision of permissible conclusion. The goal of the study is to elucidate the stylistic differences between the two periods of drama—one widely considered to have produced some of the greatest works in English, and another that is almost universally regarded as one of the low points of English literary drama. They draw a number of conclusions from their use of sophisticated statistical clustering methods, but in the end they confidently state that the sort of insight offered by George Steiner, who felt that the loss of a "redemptive worldview" had rendered Romantic tragedy an impossibility, is "well beyond the ambit of present computational stylistics" (Burrows and Craig 64).

For an algorithmic criticism to emerge, it would have to come to a philosophical decision concerning statements like these. But the question is less about agreement or disagreement, and more about a willingness to inquire into the hermeneutical foundations that make such statements seem necessary. The computer is certainly incapable of offering "the shift to a redemptive worldview" as a solution to the problem at hand; it is wholly incapable of inferring this from the data. But is it likewise the case that computational results—the data and visualizations that the computer generates when it seeks to quantize and measure textual phenomena—cannot be used to engage in the sort of discussion that might lead one to such a conclusion?

It is useful to put the question this way, because in doing so we refocus the hermeneutical problem away from the nature and limits of computation (which is mostly a matter of methodology) and move it toward consideration of the nature of the discourse in which text analysis bids participation. Burrows and Craig's statement of limitation is valid if we consider computational stylistics to be essentially a scientific pursuit, because within this hermeneutical framework it makes sense to frame conclusions in terms of what the data "allows." But in literary criticism—and here I am thinking of ordinary "paper based" literary criticism—conclusions are evaluated not in terms of what propositions the data allows, but in terms of the nature and depth of the discussions that result. The scientist is right to say that the plural of anecdote is not data, but in literary criticism an abundance of anecdote is precisely what allows discussion and debate to move forward.

Wallace's essay concerns what many consider to be Virginia Woolf's most experimental work. The novel consists of a series of monologues that trace the lives of six friends from early childhood to old age, with each monologue (beginning always with "Susan said" or "Bernard said") telling the characters' stories at seven distinct stages of their lives. They speak about different things and have different perspectives on the world, but they all speak in roughly the same manner, and do so from childhood to adulthood—employing, as one critic puts it, "the same kind of sentence rhythms and similar kinds of image patterns" throughout (Rosenthal 144). Some critics have suggested that there are differences that lie along the axis of gender or along a rift separating the more social characters from the more solitary ones, but in the end one has the sense of an overall unity running against the perspectival conceit that frames the narrative.

It is natural for a Modernist critic to pursue patterns of difference amid this apparent unity, in part because, as Wallace points out, subjectivity is a major concern for "the historic moment of Modernism." Are Woolf's individuated characters to be understood as six sides of an individual consciousness (six modalities of an idealized Modernist self?), or are we meant to read against the fiction of unity that Woolf has created by having each of these modalities assume the same stylistic voice?

It is tempting for the text analysis practitioner to view this as a problem to be solved—as if the question were rhetorically equivalent to "Who wrote *Federalist* 10?" The category error arises because we mistake questions about the properties of objects with questions about the phenomenal experience of observers. We may say that Woolf's novel "is" something or that it "does" something, but what we mean to capture is some far less concrete interpretative possibility connected with the experience of reading. We may ask "What does it mean?" but in the context of critical discourse this is often an elliptical way of saying "Can I interpret (or read) it this way?"

It is reasonable to imagine tools that can adjudicate questions about the properties of objects. Tools that can adjudicate the hermeneutical parameters of human reading experiences—tools that can tell you whether an interpretation is permissible—stretch considerably beyond the most ambitious fantasies of artificial intelligence. Calling computational tools "limited" because they cannot do this makes it sound as if they might one day evolve this capability, but it is not clear that human intelligence can make this determination objectively or consistently. We read and interpret, and we urge others to accept our readings and interpretations. Were we to strike upon a reading or interpretation so unambiguous as to remove the hermeneutical questions that arise, we would cease to refer to the activity as reading and interpretation. That we might refer to such uncontested statements as "facts" hardly bespeaks their superiority over less certain judgments.

If text analysis is to participate in literary critical endeavor in some manner beyond fact-checking, it must endeavor to assist the critic in the unfolding of interpretative possibilities. We might say that its purpose should be to generate further "evidence," though we do well to bracket the association that term holds in the context of less methodologically certain pursuits. The evidence we seek is not definitive, but suggestive of grander arguments and schemes. The "problem" (to bracket another term) with Woolf's novel is that despite evidence of a unified style, one suspects that we can read and interpret it using a set of underlying distinctions. We can uncover those distinctions by reading carefully. We can also uncover them using a computer.

It is possible—and indeed an easy matter—to use a computer to transform Woolf's novel into lists of tokens in which each list represents the words spoken by the characters ordered from most distinctive to least distinctive term. *Tf – idf,* one of the classic formulas from the field of information retrieval, endeavors to generate lists of distinctive terms for each document in a corpus. We might therefore conceive of Woolf's novel as a "corpus" of separate documents (each speaker's monologue representing a separate document), and use the formula to factor the presence of a word in a particular speaker's vocabulary against the presence of that word in the other speakers' vocabularies.

Criticism drifts into the language of mathematics. Let *tf* equal the number of times a word occurs within a single document. So, for example, if the word "a" occurred 194 times in one of the monologues, the value of *tf* would be 194. A term frequency list is therefore the set of *tf* values for each term within that speaker's vocabulary. Such lists are not without utility for certain applications, but they tend to follow patterns that are of limited usefulness for our purposes. Since the highest-frequency terms in a given document are almost always particles ("the" can account for as much as 7 percent of a corpus vocabulary), and the lower-frequency words are almost always single-instance words (or *"hapax legomena,"* as they are referred to in the field), we often end up with a list of words that is better at demonstrating the general properties of word distribution in a natural language than it is at showing us the distinctive vocabulary of an author.

If, however, we modulate the term frequency based on how ubiquitous the term is in the overall set of speakers, we can diminish the importance of terms that occur widely in the other speakers (like particles) and raise the importance of terms that are peculiar to a speaker. *Tf – idf* accomplishes this using the notion of an inverse document frequency:

$$tf - idf = tf \cdot \left(\frac{N}{df} \right)$$

Let *N* equal the total number of documents and let *df* equal the number of documents in which the target term appears. We have six speakers. If the term occurs only in one speaker, we multiply *tf* by six over one; if it occurs in all speakers, we multiply it by six over six. Thus, a word that occurs 194 times, but in all documents, is multiplied by a factor of one (six over six). A word that occurs in one document, but nowhere else, is multiplied by a factor of six (six over one).

Here are the first twenty-five lines of output from a program designed to apply the *tf* – *idf* formula to the character of Louis:[1]

Weight	Term	Weight	Term
5.917438	mr	4.2756658	disorder
5.7286577	western	3.9164972	accent
5.5176187	nile	3.7602086	beaten
5.0021615	australian	3.7602086	bobbing
5.0021615	beast	3.7602086	custard
5.0021615	grained	3.7602086	discord
5.0021615	thou	3.7602086	eating-shop
5.0021615	wilt	3.7602086	england
4.675485	pitchers	3.7602086	eyres
4.675485	steel	3.7602086	four-thirty
4.2756658	attempt	3.7602086	ham
4.2756658	average	3.7602086	lesson
4.2756658	clerks		

Few readers of *The Waves* would fail to see some emergence of pattern in this list. Many have noted that Louis seems obsessed with Egypt and the Nile. The list indicates that such terms are indeed distinctive to Louis, but the second most distinctive term in his vocabulary is the word "western." Louis is also very conscious of his accent and his nationality (he is Australian; all the other characters are English), and yet the fact that "accent" is a distinctive term for Louis would seem to indicate that the other characters aren't similarly concerned with the way he talks. Further analysis revealed that only one other character (Neville) mentions it. Louis is likewise the only character in the novel to speak of "England."

This list is a paratext that now stands alongside the other, impressing itself upon it and upon our own sense of what is meaningful. Does this "western" stand against Louis's "east"? Returning to the text, but with our focus narrowed and reframed, we discover that Louis's fondness for the words "western," "wilt," and "thou" comes from his repetition of a famous sixteenth-century poem: "Western wind, when wilt thou blow? / The small rain down can rain. / Christ, if my love were in my arms, / And I in my bed again" (*Waves* 203). Woolf quotes the poem again in the nearly contemporaneous second series of *The Common Reader* ("How Should One Read a Book?"), noting, "Who when they read these four lines stops to ask who wrote them, or conjures up the thought of Donne's house or Sidney's secretary; or enmeshes them in the intricacy of the past and the succession of generations? The poet is always our contemporary" (265).

Bernard		Louis		Neville	
thinks	rabbit	mr	clerks	catullus	loads
letter	tick	western	disorder	doomed	mallet
curiosity	tooth	nile	accent	immitigable	marvel
moffat	arrive	australian	beaten	papers	shoots
final	bandaged	beast	bobbing	bookcase	squirting
important	bowled	grained	custard	bored	waits
low	brushed	thou	discord	camel	stair
simple	buzzing	wilt	eating-shop	detect	abject
canopy	complex	pitchers	england	expose	admirable
getting	concrete	steel	eyres	hubbub	ajax
hoot	deeply	attempt	four-thirty	incredible	aloud
hums	detachment	average	ham	lack	bath

Jinny		Rhoda		Susan	
tunnel	cabinet	oblong	immune	setter	cabbages
prepared	coach	dips	many-backed	washing	carbolic
melancholy	crag	bunch	minnows	apron	clara
billowing	dazzle	fuller	pond	pear	cow
fiery	deftly	moonlight	structure	seasons	cradle
game	equipped	party	wonder	squirrel	eggs
native	eyebrows	them—	tiger	window-pane	ernest
peers	felled	allowed	swallow	kitchen	hams
quicker	frightened	cliffs	africa	baby	hare
victory	gaze	empress	amorous	betty	lettuce
band	jump	fleet	attitude	bitten	locked
banners	lockets	garland	bow	boil	maids

Similar convergences appear in the other lists (see above). For Jinny, whose relationships with men form the liminal background of her narrative, words like "billowing" (a sexually charged word almost always used in reference to her skirts), "fiery," "victory," and "dazzle" appear in the top twenty-five. For Bernard, the aspiring novelist who some say is modeled on Woolf herself, the top word is "thinks." Susan becomes a housewife and frequently invokes the virtues of a pastoral life in the country; nearly every word in her vocabulary seems directly related to the domestic. For Neville, the brilliant unrequited lover of Percival (a mutual friend of all the characters who dies while serving in India), the word "doomed" is in second place.

We might begin to wonder how vocabulary plays out along the gender axis. For example, we might modify the *tf – idf* program so that it gives us lists of words that are spoken (but shared) only by the women in the novel and another that lists words spoken only by the men. When we do that, we find that the women possess fourteen words in common:

shoes	lambert	million	pirouetting	antlers
bowl	breath	coarse	cotton	diamonds
rushes	soften	stockings	wash	

The men have ninety words in common:

boys	possible	ends	church	sentences
everybody	larpent	tortures	feeling	office
united	felt	rhythm	weep	heights
wheel	able	however	banker	accepted
hundred	brisbane	act	included	ourselves
alas	inflict	poetry	approach	irrelevant
power	background	knew	arms	baker
language	destiny	banks	latin	letters
became	meeting	lord	block	neat
poet	board	novel	reason	brake
observe	respect	burnt	oppose	telephone
central	pointing	waistcoat	certainly	sensations
beak	chose	sheer	chaos	cinders
story	difficult	clamour	suffering	endure
course	torture	forgotten	crucifix	troubling
friend	distinctions	use	god	distracted
waste	king	doctor	watched	notice
ease	willows	ordinary	edges	works

These are provocative results, but the provocation is as much about our sense of what we are doing (the hermeneutical question) as it is about how we are doing it (the methodological question).

We might want to say that the purpose of these procedures is to confirm or deny the "serendipitous reading" of literary critics. Is Louis obsessed with his accent? Yes; the data confirms that he is. Critics who have argued for a deep structure of difference among the characters—one perhaps aligned along the gender axis—might also feel as if the program vindicates their impressions. Is there a gender divide? Yes; the characters are divided along the gender axis by a factor of 6.4285 to 1.

To level such arguments, however, is to turn the hermeneutical question back into a methodological one. To speak of the procedure as "verifying" some other finding is to beg questions of the procedure itself. And here, we are on somewhat shaky ground. The formula $tf - idf$ "works" in the context of information retrieval because it appears to match our general expectations. When we undertake a search for the term "baseball" with a search engine, we want to rule out passing references in favor of documents that are substantially about this topic. If we get back relevant hits, we could say that the $tf - idf$ formula has done its job. In the case of Woolf, we might say that we are getting back results that conform to our general expectations of what distinguishes the characters. But $tf - idf$ itself has no more claim to truth value than any ordinary reading procedure. Manning and Schütze, in their magisterial work on statistical natural language processing, note that the "the family of *[tf – idf]* weighting schemes is sometimes criticized because it is not directly derived from a mathematical model of term distribution or relevancy" (544). The full version of the formula (the one used to generate the results above) includes a *log* function and an addition:

$$tf - idf = 1 + tf \cdot \log\left(\frac{N}{df}\right)$$

The main purpose of these additions is not to bring the results into closer conformity with "reality," but merely to render the weighting numbers more sensible to the analyst. The logarithm dampens the function so that one term isn't a full six times more important than another; the +1 keeps the end of the curve from trailing off into negative territory.

Some text-analytical procedures do rely on empirical facts about language (or on statistical and mathematical laws in general). But even when they do, we often find ourselves unable to point to the truth of the procedure as the basis for judgment. We might say that this is because literary criticism is insufficiently scientific. We might even long for a "scientific literary criticism." We would do better to recognize that a scientific literary criticism would cease to be criticism.

It is no longer controversial to point out that science involves interpretation, rhetoric, social construction, and politics—as if this exposure of science's hidden humanism could somehow discredit the achievements of one of the world's greatest epistemological tools. No serious scientist could ever deny that interpretation, disagreement, and debate is at the core of the scientific method. But science differs significantly from the humanities in that it seeks singular answers to the problems under discussion. However far ranging a scientific debate might be, however varied the interpretations being offered, the assumption remains that there is a singular answer (or a singular set of answers) to the question at hand. Literary criticism has no such assumption. In the humanities the fecundity of any particular discussion is often judged precisely by the degree to which it offers ramified solutions to the problem at hand. We are not trying to solve Woolf. We are trying to ensure that discussion of *The Waves* continues.

Critics often use the word "pattern" to describe what they're putting forth, and that word aptly connotes the fundamental nature of the data upon which literary insight relies. The understanding promised by the critical act arises not from a presentation of facts, but from the elaboration of a gestalt, and it rightfully includes the vague reference, the conjectured similitude, the ironic twist, and the dramatic turn. In the spirit of *inventio,* the critic freely employs the rhetorical tactics of conjecture—not so that a given matter might be definitely settled, but in order that the matter might become richer, deeper, and ever more complicated. The proper response to the conundrum posed by Steiner's "redemptive worldview" is not the scientific imperative toward verification and falsification, but the humanistic propensity toward disagreement and elaboration.

If algorithmic criticism is to have a central hermeneutical tenet, it is this: that the narrowing constraints of computational logic—the irreducible tendency of the computer toward enumeration, measurement, and verification—is fully compatible with the goals of criticism set forth above. For while it is possible, and in some cases useful, to confine algorithmic procedures to the scientific realm, such procedures can be made to conform to the methodological project of *inventio* without transforming the nature of computation or limiting the rhetorical range of critical inquiry. This is possible because critical reading practices already contain elements of the algorithmic.

Any reading of a text that is not a recapitulation of that text relies on a heuristic of radical transformation. The critic who endeavors to put forth a "reading" puts forth not the text, but a new text in which the data has been paraphrased, elaborated, selected, truncated, and transduced. This basic property of critical methodology is evident not only in the act of "close reading" but also in the more ambitious project of thematic exegesis. In the classroom one encounters the professor instructing his or her students to turn to page 254, and then to page 16, and finally to page 400. They are told to consider just the male characters, or just the female ones, or to pay attention to the adjectives, the rhyme scheme, images of water, or the moment in which Nora Helmer confronts her husband. The interpreter will set a novel against the background of the Jacobite Rebellion, or a play amid the historical location of the theater. He or she will view the text through the lens of Marxism, or psychoanalysis, or existentialism, or postmodernism. In every case, what is being read is not the "original" text, but a text transformed and transduced into an alternative vision, in which, as Wittgenstein put it, we "see an aspect" that further enables discussion and debate.

It is not that such matters as redemptive worldviews and Marxist readings of texts can be arrived at algorithmically, but simply that algorithmic transformation can provide the alternative visions that give rise to such readings. The computer does this in a particularly useful way by carrying out transformations in a rigidly holistic manner. It is one thing to notice patterns of vocabulary, variations in line length, or images of darkness and light; it is another thing to employ a machine that can unerringly discover every instance of such features across a massive corpus of literary texts and then present those features in a visual format entirely foreign to the original organization in which these features appear. Or rather, it is the same thing at a different scale and with expanded powers of observation. It is in such results that the critic seeks not facts, but patterns. And from pattern the critic may move to the grander rhetorical formations that constitute critical reading.

It might still make sense to speak of certain matters being "beyond the ambit of present computational stylistics." Research in text analysis continues to seek new ways to isolate features and present novel forms of organization. But the ambit of these ways and forms need not be constrained by a hermeneutics that disallows the connotative and analogical methods of criticism. Algorithmic criticism would have to retain the commitment to methodological rigor demanded by its tools, but the emphasis would be less on maintaining a correspondence or a fitness between method and goal and more on the need to present methods in a fully transparent manner. It would not be averse to the idea of reproducibility, but it would perhaps be even more committed to the notion of "hackability." For just as one might undertake a feminist reading of a text by transporting a set of heuristics from one critical context to another, so might the algorithmic critic undertake a particular type of reading by transforming a procedure that has been defined in terms of that most modern text, the computer program.

Algorithmic criticism undoubtedly requires a revolution of sorts, but that revolution is not one of new procedures and methods in contradistinction to the old ones. Algorithmic criticism seeks a new kind of audience for text analysis—one that is less concerned with fitness of method and the determination of interpretative boundaries, and one more concerned with evaluating the robustness of the discussion that a particular procedure annunciates. Such an audience exists, of course, and has existed for the better part of a century in the general community of literary critics from which text analysis has often found itself exiled. For this reason, text analysis practitioners should view the possibility of such a revolution as both welcome and liberating—not a critique of their methods, but a bold vote of confidence in the possibilities they hold.

2 POTENTIAL LITERATURE

The word "algorithm" is an odd neologism. Most scholars now believe that the word relates back to the word "algorism," which is in turn a corruption of the name of the Persian mathematician al-Kwārizmī from whose book, *Kitāb al-jabr wa'l-muqābala* ("Rules for Restoring and Equating"), we get the word "algebra" (Knuth 1). Throughout its varied history, the term has more or less always borne the connotation of a method for solving some problem, and, as the early slide from sibilant to aspirate would imply, that problem was most often considered mathematical in nature. During the twentieth century, however, the word "algorithm" came to be associated with computers—a step-by-step method for solving a problem using a machine. To speak of algorithms is therefore usually to speak of unerring processes and irrefragable answers.

If computational methods are to be useful in the context of literary study, however, we must consider the use of algorithms loosed from the strictures of the irrefragable and explore the possibilities of a science that can operate outside of the confines of the denotative. Historically, such ventures have been viewed with deep distrust:

> The rise of scientific logic seems, indeed, to have had the effect of pushing back the ever-encroaching forces of dialectical invention into the margins of charlatanism and mental tricks. Descartes's position was clear: he insisted on clarity against quackery. . . . In the new scientific age, rhetoric's calculating genius seemed antithetical to the search for truth. Rhetoric's technologies were too random, its underlying ethos too inauthentic and artificial to contribute to a reliable description of man and the world. (Bold 544)

The Cartesian legacy, in addition to valorizing science as the sine qua non of human inquiry, had the additional effect of validating the Athenian senate's perception of philosophy as "making the weaker argument defeat the stronger" (Plato 5). Today, "rhetoric has been shown to be at the basis of what is called scientific 'method' in all but the Cartesian sense of the word," and yet the separation of these two faculties has persisted, and the trace of this once bitter opposition maintained (Bold 544).

The reverberations of this divergence are evident in the computing humanist's ironic distrust of inventions borne of algorithmic processes. Few commentators, in fact, have been able to resist framing the movement from data to interpretation as one fraught with peril. Hugh Craig, an expert in stylometry and authorship attribution, is unusually candid in an assessment that bears the subtitle, "If You Can Tell Authors Apart, Have You Learned Anything about Them?"

> The leap from frequencies to meanings must always be a risky one. The interpreter who is tempted to speculate about the world-view or psychology of a writer, based on quantitative findings, presents an easy target for dismissive critique (Fish, 1973). On the other hand, staying within the safe confines of the statistical results themselves means that one is soon left with only banalities or tautologies. Lower-level features are easy to count but impossible to interpret in terms of style; counting images or other high-level structures brings problems of excessive intervention at the categorization stage, and thus unreliability and circularity (Van Peer, 1989). (Craig 103–4)

Thus "quantitative findings" emerge, under the cultural burden of science, as entirely opposed to the imaginative work of speculation and intervention. The age-old charges against *inventio* reemerge. Without grounding in the language game of denotation, we risk the "circular reasoning" of a discourse that grounds itself in further discourse—the "unreliability" of a claim that has nothing to recommend it but its rhetorical power to persuade. Larger debates are aliased through Craig's ingenuous observations about risk, and those debates largely ignore the conundrum he identifies. C. P. Snow's 1959 Rede Lecture, "The Two Cultures and Scientific Revolution"—often cited as having put forth the essential terms of the debate between science and the humanities—figures the dichotomy as a kind of misunderstanding. If literary intellectuals (whom Snow refers to as "natural Luddites") would learn more about science and scientists would learn more about "imaginative experience," we would not only enrich the episteme of academic culture, but we would also go further toward communicating the meaning of that culture to the larger world (23). But what to do with a scholar like Craig, who is assuredly not a Luddite, and who can lay claim to having both methodologies well in hand?

To the degree that algorithmic criticism tries to enter this debate, it does so by considering a third culture that is at once the product of both scientific and artistic investigation and has subtly suffused both cultures since the turn of the twentieth century. It begins with the "'pataphysics" of Alfred Jarry, and in particular with that extraordinary "neo-scientific" novel *Gestes et opinions du docteur Faustroll, pataphysicien,* in which the science of "imaginary solutions" is put forth.

Faustroll is by any measure a baffling and inscrutable work. Its conventional status as the ur-text of Absurdism might indeed tempt us to seek no meaning in it beyond the philosophical implications of its emphatic rejection of realistic portrayals and narrative forms. It describes a journey, but one that takes the main character "from Paris to Paris by Sea" (Jarry 177); characters die, but only "provisionally"; there are dialogues, but one character is incapable of saying anything other than "Ha ha"; there are epistolary passages, but the letters are delivered telepathically; proofs are offered, but they establish God as "the tangential point between zero and infinity" (256). In the context of this beguiling tale, the declaration of a new science would seem, at best, satirical. This view, however, obscures the seriousness of the intellectual provocation that lies at the center of *Faustroll:* the illumination of a philosophical point of intersection between scientific and imaginative endeavor.

More than three-quarters of the novel is framed as a dunning letter written by Rene-Isidore Panmuphle, bailiff. We are to understand, though the sense of this context is quickly obscured, that most of the novel is a narrative appended to a "summons Pursuant to Article 819," duly sealed as an "official paper" of a law court:

> I, the undersigned, Rene-Isidore Panmuphle, Bailiff attached to the Civil Court of First Instance of the Department of Seine, in session at Paris, residing in said City, 37, rue Pavee, Do hereby summon in the name of the LAW and of JUSTICE, Monsieur Faustroll, doctor, tenant of various premises dependent upon the house aforementioned, residing at Paris, 100 bis, rue Richer, and having proceeded to the aforementioned house, bearing upon its exterior the number 100, and having rung, knocked, and called the aforementioned variously and successively, no person having opened the door to us, and the next door neighbors declaring to us that this is indeed the residence of said M. Faustroll. (Jarry 182)[1]

Faustroll thus begins in the realm of the denotative—nearly two pages of introductory clauses appended to the phrase "he shall be constrained thereto" (182). With such legalese, Jarry illustrates the poverty that language assumes when strained to the breaking point of an unattainable precision. Immediately following this farcical attempt to constrain the possibilities of language, Panmuphle discovers in Faustroll's apartment twenty-seven "equivalent books" ranging from Coleridge's *The Rime of the Ancient Mariner* to *The Gospel According to St. Luke* (in Greek). The language of restriction gives way to a vision of language so permeated with possibility that one may argue (as Jarry does) that texts as apparently disparate as those enumerated might be recast as versions of the same underlying narrative.

The journey that ensues is not so much from place to place as from text to text—or, more accurately, a journey from place to place where the places are Jarry's transformations of textual/imaginative space into geographical space (Stillman, *Alfred Jarry* 22). Such swings, from the imaginative possibilities of the literal to the literal possibilities of the imaginative, characterize the general movement of the novel. In the midst of these surreal imaginings, however, Faustroll breaks in with a moment of extreme clarity—the enunciation of the new science of 'pataphysics:

> definition. 'Pataphysics is the science of imaginary solutions, which symbolically attributes the properties of objects, described by their virtuality, to their lineaments.
>
> Contemporary science is founded upon the principle of induction: most people have seen a certain phenomenon precede or follow some other phenomenon most often, and conclude therefrom that it will ever be thus. Apart from other considerations, this is true only in the majority of cases, depends upon the point of view, and is codified only for convenience—if that! Instead of formulating the law of the fall of a body toward a center, how far more apposite would be the law of the ascension of a vacuum toward a periphery, a vacuum being considered a unit of non-density, a hypothesis far less arbitrary than the choice of a concrete unit of positive density such as water? (Jarry 193)

At its most fundamental level, 'pataphysics is the apotheosis of perspectivalism—a mode, not of inquiry, but of *being,* which refuses to see the relativity of perspective as a barrier to knowledge. For Jarry, the fact that "Questions always define in advance the regime of their answers" opens up the possibility of an epistemology utterly freed from the confines of the denotative (Bök 28).

For Jarry, science requires the process of ascribing the lineaments of perspectival vision to the virtuality of imaginative vision. Without such anarchic vision, the scientist becomes inured to the possibilities of exception—a victim of common consent and habit: "Universal assent is already a quite miraculous and incomprehensible prejudice. Why should anyone claim that the shape of a watch is round—a manifestly false proposition—since it appears in profile as a narrow rectangular construction, elliptic on three sides; and why the devil should one only have noticed its shape at the moment of looking at the time?" (193). If scientific knowledge is borne of 'pataphysical seeings, those seeings likewise aspire to a different epistemological category—not the metaphysical light under which science operates, but "that which is superinduced upon metaphysics, whether within or beyond the latter's limitations, extending as far beyond metaphysics as the latter extends beyond physics" (192). In contrast to metaphysical understanding, 'pataphysical understanding cannot be contradicted or superseded by alternative visions. As Christian Bök describes it, 'pataphysics bespeaks "not the terrorism of unified theories but the anarchism of ramified theories . . . a savoir-faire economy (whose Lucretian arbitration requires that nomad science bracket the truth of a defunct concept as either dormant or defiant)" (25).

Bök correctly intuits the continuities between Jarry's critique and the anarchic science of Feyerabend:

> Feyerabend argues that, for science to progress, the nomic truth of the *as is* must induce an escape to the ludic space of an *as if*: *"we need a dreamworld in order to discover the features of the real world . . . which may actually be just another dream world"* (Feyerabend 32). . . . 'Pataphysics dramatizes this principle of Feyerabend by arguing that however obsolete or indiscreet any theory might at first appear, every theory has the potential to improve knowledge in some way. Just as biodiversity can make an ecology more adaptable, so can dilettantism make an episteme more versatile. The process of science must learn to place its defunct concepts into a kind of suspended animation that preserves them for the millenary reverie of an imaginary science. The truth diverges through many truths, inducing sophisms of dissent, novelty, and paradox: "given any rule . . . for science, there are always circumstances when it is advisable not only to ignore the rule, but to adopt its opposite" (Feyerabend 32). (Bök 25)

The narrative of *Faustroll* is everywhere sustained by the sophisms of dissent, novelty, and paradox. It is inscrutable and anti-realistic because, as Linda Klieger Stillman has observed, "the imaginary hypothesis replaces the known or the probable and insinuates itself into the order of things as reality. The texts' constantly shifting perspectives establish the possible, rather than the probable, as credible" (*Alfred Jarry* 16).

All of this might seem beside the point—an artistic reverie unallied with the practical concerns of experimental science. But the same insinuations that characterize the imaginative lucubrations of 'pataphysics likewise capture a genre and method of inquiry that has come to characterize modern scientific inquiry. Beginning in the nineteenth century, the nomic drive of scientific speculation began sowing the seeds of a revolutionary cosmology populated with particles smaller than the *atomos,* universes alternative (and supplementary) to our own, and peculiar convergences between energy and matter. In the light of such marvels, we witness modern science turning to narrative—not merely as a way to explain complex phenomena, but as a methodology for exploring the meaning and implication of phenomena. While Jarry was formulating his new science, the scientist-turned-philosopher Ernst Mach was coining the term "thought experiment" to describe these new meditations.[2]

For Kuhn, the thought experiment was "one of the essential analytic tools which are deployed during crisis and which then help to promote basic conceptual reform" (263). The most famous examples of the genre demonstrate the radical difference between such experiments and the attendant genres of illustration and exemplar. Maxwell's demon does not illustrate the Second Law of Thermodynamics, but instead attempts to imagine a universe in which the law cannot hold. Schrödinger's cat likewise provides not an example of the principle of superposition in quantum mechanics, but an instance in which the principle appears flatly absurd. In both cases, the narrative amounts to an impossible fantasy constructed for the purpose of divining the possibilities of the real. In a sense, thought experiment is the hyperbolic extreme of reductio ad absurdam—the 'pataphysical expansion of reality to the point of absurdity, which, like the ancient *reductio,* has truth as its ultimate object. Jarry's awareness of the narrative possibilities of such experiments are everywhere apparent in *Faustroll.* It is not at all fortuitous that Lucretius, the source from which Jarry borrowed some of the important terminology of 'pataphysics (e.g., *clinamen),* is likewise the source of one of the earliest and most elegant instances of thought experiment in Western science. More convincing still, however, are the ways in which the use of scientific narrative provides the framework for so much of Faustroll's journey.

Many critics have attempted to catalog the numerous texts that inspire Faustroll's odyssey.[3] Much of the novel, in fact, may be conceived as Jarry's 'pataphysical transformation of existing works. Coincident with these literary journeys, however, is a set of important late-century scientific texts culled from the writings of Lord Kelvin, William Crookes, and Charles Vernon Boys—writings that, unlike the literary exemplars, permeate the entire structure of *Faustroll.*[4] Faustroll's sieve, which floats upon the water despite being perforated with holes, comes more or less directly from Boys's *Soap Bubbles: Their Colours and the Forces Which Mould Them* (1890):

> I have a small sieve made of wire gauze sufficiently coarse to allow a common pin to be put through any of the holes. There are moreover about eleven thou-

sand of these holes in the bottom of the sieve. . . . Dip the sieve in hot paraffin, shake to knock out of the holes. . . . Water goes through only if forced . . . therefore, it has an elastic skin which requires force to stretch. If now I shake the water off the sieve I can set it to float on water, because its weight is not sufficient to stretch the skin of the water through all the holes. You see that it is quite possible to go to sea in a sieve—that is, if the sieve is large enough and the water is not too rough. (Boys, qtd. in Stillman, "Physics" 90)

Thus Jarry uses the science of Boys to explore the realistic possibilities of a nonsense poem (Lear's "The Jumblies") (Lear 71–74).

One of the most impressive passages in *Faustroll* is an imaginative fantasia on a theme drawn from a speech given by William Crookes and published in *Presidential Addresses to the Society for Psychical Research 1882–1911*. There, Crookes proposes to address "those who not only take too terrestrial a view, but who deny the plausibility—nay, the possibility—of the existence of an unseen world at all . . . the world of the infinitely little" (qtd. in Stillman, *Alfred Jarry* 85). Crookes proposed that we imagine a homunculus perched on a cabbage leaf. For this creature, the molecular forces that govern surface tension and elasticity "occur amidst a burst of sound and light" (Stillman, "Physics" 85), thus enabling us to apprehend these forces more clearly. Faustroll, true to form, wishes to experience this radical change in perspective firsthand:

For this purpose he chose the substance which is normally liquid, colorless, incompressible and horizontal in small quantities; having a curved surface, blue in depth and with edges that tend to ebb and flow when it is stretched; which Aristotle terms heavy, like earth; the enemy of fire and renascent from it when decomposed explosively; which vaporizes at a hundred degrees, a temperature determined by this fact, and in a solid state floats upon itself—water, of course! And having shrunk along the length of a cabbage leaf, paying no attention to his fellow mites or the magnified aspect of his surroundings, until he encountered the Water.

This was a globe, twice his size, through whose transparency the outlines of the universe appeared to him gigantically enlarged, whilst his own image, reflected dimly by the leaves' foil was magnified to his original size. He gave the orb a light rap, as if knocking on a door: the deracinated eye of malleable glass "adapted itself" like a living eye, became presbyopic, lengthened itself along its horizontal diameter into an ovoid myopia, repulsed Faustroll by means of this elastic inertia and became spherical once more.

The doctor, taking small steps, rolled the crystal globe, with some considerable difficulty, toward a neighboring globe, slipping on the rails of the cabbage-leaf's veins; coming together, the two spheres sucked each other in, tapering in the process, until suddenly a new globe of twice the size rocked placidly in front of Faustroll.

With the tip of his boot the doctor kicked out at this unexpected development of the elements: an explosion, formidable in its fragmentation and noise, rang out following the projection all around of new and minute spheres, dry and hard as diamonds, that rolled to and fro all along the green arena, each one drawing along beneath it the image of the tangential point of the universe, distorting it according to the sphere's projection and magnifying its fabulous center. (Jarry 194–95)

This extraordinary passage is more philosophy of science than science fiction. The defamiliarization proposed by the alternative vision of science—the presbyopia and myopia of 'pataphysical exception—leads to an imaginative vision in which the "fabulous center" of the object is magnified. Crookes uses the figure to explain; Jarry, to enact the imaginative facility that led to the original insight.

Imaginative use of the tools of science characterizes nearly all the movements that claim 'pataphysics as its patrimony. If Jarry's work anticipates the age of Heisenberg, Oulipo—perhaps the grandest and most enduring of the 'pataphysical descendants—represents a refraction of the age of Gödel. Oulipo, indeed, might be said to do with (and for) mathematics and structural linguistics what Jarry did with physics: use the terms of its vision in order to seek not denotative truth, but imaginative insight.

For Oulipo, that imaginative meaning arises at the intersection of *potentiality* and *constraint*. The former represents the most obvious continuity with 'pataphysics. For Jacques Bens (one of the founding members of the group), it is one of the features that place the Oulipo within the context of a modernity entirely distinct from the idle formalism of past movements: "And now, if one begins to consider that potentiality, more than a technique of composition, is a certain way of conceiving the literary object, it would perhaps be allowed that the idea of potentiality opens into a perfectly authentic modern realism. Since reality never reveals more than a part of its totality, it thereby justifies a thousand interpretations, significations, and solutions, all equally probable" (Bens, qtd. in Thomas 20).[5] Oulipo thus approaches the literary work as Jarry approaches the watch face—as an object rife with exceptions, brimming with paths not taken and possibilities unexplored.

The earliest works of the Oulipo tended to dramatize this notion by illustrating the combinatorial properties of literary forms. Raymond Queneau's *Cent Mille Milliards de Poems* (*100,000,000,000,000 Poems*), generally considered the inaugural work of the group, consists of a sequence of ten sonnets (each a coherent work) arranged in such a way that one may interchange lines from each of the different sonnets to create a new sonnet.[6] The mathematical properties of the book—which are no less astonishing for being easy to explain—are a major discursive element of the work. If there are ten possibilities for the first line, and any one of those lines may be followed by one of ten additional lines, it follows that the number of possible combinations is 10×10 (or $10^2 = 100$). Since that number will increase by a factor of ten with each additional line, a fourteen-line poem becomes, in its potential state, the Cartesian product of its sets: i.e., 10^{14} (100 trillion) possibilities. Queneau determined that a person reading the book twenty-four hours a day would need 190,258,751 years to finish it (Mathews and Brotchie 14).

In the midst of this combinatorial explosion, however, lies the rigid constraint of form. As one critic has noted, "The sonnets are executed with a fine attention to detail, and in a manner which implicitly valorizes the process, as well as the product; in a word, they are craftsmanlike" (Motte, "Raymond Queneau" 201). The craftsmanship of each poem, moreover, extends to the concinnity necessary for facilitating combination with the other poems. The result is "a smoothly-functional machine for the production and dissemination of literature" (203)—literature that declares its potentiality not in spite of, but because of the constraints imposed.

Here is the second sonnet in Stanley Chapman's translation of the work:

The wild horse champs the Parthenon's top frieze
Since Elgin left his nostrils in the stone
The Turks said just take anything you please
And loudly sang off-key without a tone
O Parthenon you hold the charger's strings
The North Wind bites into his architrave
Th'outrageous Thames a troubled arrow slings
To break a rule Britannia's might might waive
Platonic Greece was not so talentless
A piercing wit would sprightliest horses flog
Socrates watched his hemlock effervesce
Their sculptors did *our* best our hulks they clog
With marble souvenirs then fill a slum
For Europe's glory while Fate's harpies strum.
                    (Mathews and Brotchie 17)

Here is a poem (of my own, and perhaps also Queneau's, creation) using that poem and the other nine from the sequence:

The wild horse champs the Parthenon's top frieze
His nasal ecstasy beats best Cologne
He bent right down and well what did he seize
The thumb- and finger-prints of Al Capone

How it surprised us pale grey underlings
When flame a form to wrath ancestral gave
Proud death quite il-le-gi-ti-mate-ly stings
Etruscan words which Greece and Rome engrave
Poetic license needs no strain or stress
With gravity at gravity's great cog
Watching manure and compost coalesce
Their sculptors did *our* best our hulks they clog
With marble souvenirs then fill a slum
A wise loaf always knows its humblest crumb

One does not so much write a Queneauian sonnet as implement one using the formal constraints of the work. Though one might create a poem using random selections, the physical arrangement discourages this approach. Jacque Bens, in fact, considered avoidance of randomness a defining characteristic of the group: "The members of the Oulipo have never hidden their abhorrence of the aleatory, of bogus fortunetellers and penny-ante lotteries" (qtd. in Motte, *Oulipo* 17). Rather, one consciously and deliberately looks for interesting combinations of lines and poetic effects. In building my sonnet, I found myself unable to resist the urge to make the wild horse of the Elgin marbles seize "the thumb- and finger-prints of Al Capone." I was similarly delighted at how "pale grey underlings," though taken from a completely different poem, seemed to harmonize with the marble motif; likewise "Greece and Rome" with the Parthenon, "manure" with horses, and "nasal ecstasy" with the image of a horse champing at the bit. One has the clear sense of having discovered something with these combinations—of having liberated certain energies in the work—while at the same time having beat Queneau at his own game.

Queneau's unusual sonnet sequence bears an obvious resemblance to the Dadaist technique of cutting up poems and reassembling them into new formations, but there is little of the anti-art rhetoric of Tzara in Queneau's work. Tzara's poems seek to destroy; Queneau's to create. The Surrealists, echoing mythologies both of the Muse and of the artist as a conduit of "musical" energy and truthfulness, tended to stress the inspirational aspect of poetic creation. The Oulipians, by contrast, emphasize the original sense of poiesis as a "making" or "building." For Queneau, who sought to renounce his earlier affiliations with Breton and the Surrealists, "La littérateur est l'artiste et l'artiste est artisan" (Queneau 95). Constraint, which might at first seem to oppose the exuberant perspectivalism of potentiality, reveals itself in the work of the Oulipo as the condition under which perspective shifts and potential emerges. The constraints of form—like the strictures of scientific and mathematical reasoning—alter one's vision and expose the explosive potentiality of the subject and of subjectivity. Without such alterations, writing cannot break out of its conventions. "Often, the Oulipo proposes [its constraints] freely to other writers who are, one imagines, beached, blocked, brutalized by the false prophets of genius and inspiration" (Motte, "Raymond Queneau" 203).

Few Oulipian works illustrate the liberation of constraint as well as Walter Abish's *Alphabetical Africa* (1974), which uses a series of seemingly impossible strictures to construct a coherent prose narrative.[7] The first chapter permits only the use of words that begin with the letter "a"; the second with the letters "a," "b"; the third with "a," "b," or "c"; and so on until the full range of letters have been employed, at which point the process reverses itself. The novel begins, "Ages ago, Alex, Allen and Alva arrived at Antibes, and Alva allowing all, allowing anyone, against Alex's admonition, against Allen's angry assertion: another African amusement." (1). Chapter 2 begins, "Before African adjournment, Alex, Allen and Alva arrive at Antibes, beginning a big bash, as August brings back a buoyancy, a belief, Ahh, and believing all buy books about Angolan basins and about Burundi bathhouses." (3). Anthony Schirato, who sees in Abish's work both a comic parody and a critique of Western imperialism, adroitly isolates the ways in which the constraints of the novel's form impel the novelty of its revolution: "Angolan attacks, Dogon destructions, and Eritrean erasures occur precisely because the alphabetical rules within which the text operates preclude much opportunity for anything but largely undifferentiated and often repetitious descriptions. African anthills are attacked in the first 'A' chapter; Angolans can be bombed in chapter 'B' and suffer death in chapter 'D,' but until chapter 'S,' they, of course, cannot suffer at all" (135). The intelligibility of Abish's text—which, as Schirato demonstrates, extends to the richness of political metaphor—is not a fortuitous accident of its form, but a direct result of its constraints. As Jarry asks (of the objects of reality) what infinite smallness would entail, so Abish's text asks what narrative might emerge from a text in which no one can "die" until chapter 4 or "suffer" until chapter 19.

In the earlier chapters of the work, the emergence of convincing narrative from these strictures is perhaps the foremost feature, but the most astonishing chapter of all is surely the twenty-sixth, where the author allows himself the full use of the alphabet:

> Zambia helps fill our zoos, and our doubts, and our extra-wide screens as we
> sit back. Each year we zigzag between the cages, prodding the alligators, the
> antelopes, the giant ants, just to see them move about a bit, just to make our
> life more authentic, help us recapture the fantasy we had while watching the

wide-screen spectacular with rock Hudson on horseback, or the African Queen zapping Panda the wild leopard. I stayed in Africa for a few weeks. Took the tours. Met a few people. (Abish 64)

It is almost impossible to read this paragraph, after the previous twenty-five chapters, without an awareness of the first letters of the words—of the rich liberation of writing. It is perhaps the only passage in all of English prose that is notable for the *absence* of alliteration (if that is even the right term for the effect).

Queneau's work demonstrates the generative qualities of form; Abish's, the performative qualities of that generation. Together, the two procedures represent a large category of Oulipian forms. There is, however, a third type that represents the most obvious literary analogue to computer-assisted criticism—namely, poetry generated by purely algorithmic processes. One of the most famous of these is the so-called Mathews algorithm, which remaps the data structure of a set of linguistic units (letters of words, lines of poems, paragraphs of novels) into a two-dimensional tabular array. We might begin with four four-letter words arranged like so:[8]

```
T    I    N    E
S    A    L    E
M    A    L    E
V    I    N    E
```
(tine, sale, male, vine)

The characters in each row are then shifted $n - 1$ places to the left, and new words are formed by reading the letters downward in the columns (beginning with the initial letter from the previous row):

```
T    I    N    E
A    L    E    S
L    E    M    A
E    V    I    N
```
(tale, vile, mine, sane)

Next, the words are shifted to the right in the same manner and the results read upward:

```
T    I    N    E
E    S    A    L
L    E    M    A
I    N    E    V
```
(tile, sine, mane, vale)

These maneuvers thus create a serendipitous morphology—an instantiation of the phonemic potentiality of ordinary words.

The same procedure may be undertaken with tables formed from words, phrases, sentences, or any other identifiable linguistic unit. Here is an example of a poem formed from a table of quatrains and couplets taken from Shakespeare, Herbert, Jonson, and Donne:

> Farewell! thou art too dear for my possessing,
> And like enough thou know'st thy estimate:
> The charter of thy worth gives thee releasing,
> My bonds in thee are all determinate,
> While mortal love doth all the title gain!
> Which sliding with invention, they together
> Bear all the sway, possessing heart and brain
> (Thy workmanship) and give thee share in neither.
> But now thy work is done, if they that view
> The several figures languish in suspense
> to judge which passion's false, and which is true,
> Between the doubtful sway of reason and sense;
> That thou remember them, some claim as debt;
> I think it mercy if thou wilt forget.
>
> (Motte, *Oulipo* 134)

For Mathews, the notion of potentiality in literature consists in the realization that alternative textualities "lie in wait to subvert and perhaps surpass" the original formation (126). "The fine surface unity that a piece of writing proposes is belied and beleaguered; behind it, in the realm of potentiality, a dialectic has emerged" (126). The algorithm therefore represents "a new means of tracking down this otherness hidden in language (and, perhaps, in what language talks about)" (126). Form, in other words, is both a means of poetic communication and an enunciation of possible procedures for analyzing that communication.

On the one hand, the hybrid sonnet is a work of poetic artifice—a new poem created, like all poems, from previous instances of language. Yet this same act has the effect of highlighting certain formal dimensions of the poem that we usually associate with critical observation. We might expect an artful nonsense to emerge; instead, we get a poem that, if not perfectly coherent, is at least mimicking the aural dimension of sensefulness. As a critical work, the new poem makes obvious a long-standing critical intuition about sonnet form—namely, that the form itself has a rhetorical structure that is almost independent of the words themselves, insofar as the form raises expectations that may condition us to pursue particular patterns of sense making. We expect a sonnet to "turn," to engage in a certain call-and-response pattern between octave and sestet, perhaps to resolve with an ironic (or witty, or playful) couplet. Those expectations compel us to create sense even from lines that literally have nothing to do with one another. The hybrid poem is therefore not just a hybrid of various sonnets, but, with the addition of the algorithm, a hybrid between poetical and critical acts. It is not entirely cogent to call the poem "an interpretation," if we also intend that term to signify language acts like the paragraph above this one. At the same time, the algorithmic manipulation that produced the text would seem to problematize our desire to consider it a purely poetical or creative act, if we also intend that term to signify language acts like the original sonnets that make up the new formation.

'Pataphysics, Oulipian constraint, and the tradition of thought experiment all gesture toward a critical vanishing point at which the distinctions between art, criticism, and science dissolve. At the practical level, these distinctions remain firm: Jarry's lucubrations are not science, just as Crooke's fantasias are not those of an artist. Yet the artist and the scientist both endeavor to place the phenomenal world into some alternative formation that will facilitate a new seeing. Computation, particularly as it inserts itself into fields like bioinformatics or computational physics, manifests itself in much the same way as it does (naturally, almost inexorably) in the work of the Oulipo—as something both new and old, provocative and stabilizing, threatening and comforting. The computer revolutionizes, not because it proposes an alternative to the basic hermeneutical procedure, but because it reimagines that procedure at new scales, with new speeds, and among new sets of conditions. It is for this reason that one can even dare to imagine such procedures taking hold in a field like literary criticism.

3 POTENTIAL READINGS

"Algorithmic criticism"—the term I use to designate a reconceived computer-assisted literary criticism—shares with Oulipo a desire to use the narrowing forces of constraint to enable the liberating visions of potentiality. Its medium is the computer, but it looks neither to the bare calculating facilities of the mechanism nor to the promise of machine intelligence for its inspiration. Instead, algorithmic criticism attempts to employ the rigid, inexorable, uncompromising logic of algorithmic transformation as the constraint under which critical vision may flourish. The hermeneutic proposed by algorithmic criticism does not oppose the practice of conventional critical reading, but instead attempts to reenvision its logics in extreme and self-conscious forms. As such, it is of a piece with recent work on the notion of "textual intervention" as set forth by Rob Pope; of "deformance" as proposed by Jerome McGann and Lisa Samuels; and with the computationally enacted "tamperings" undertaken by Estelle Irizarry. All three set forth a bold heuresis—one that proposes not a radical exegesis, but a radical *eisegesis* (perhaps a *katagesis)* in which the graphic and semantic codes of textuality are deliberately and literally altered.

Pope's 1994 *Textual Intervention* is to criticism what *The Oulipo Compendium* is to poetry—not primarily a theoretical exposition, but a textbook full of problems, exercises, and worked examples. Were we to insert references to computation, its opening preface might serve not only as a description of algorithmic criticism but also as a general motto for much of what we already call digital humanities:

> The best way to understand how a text works, I argue, is to change it: to play around with it, to intervene in it in some way (large or small), and then to try

to account for the exact effect of what you have done. In practice—not just in theory—we have the option of making changes at all levels, from the merest nuance of punctuation or intonation to total recasting in terms of genre, time, place, participants and medium. . . . The emphasis throughout is on exploring possible permutations and realizations of texts in and out of their original contexts. (Pope 1)

To ask "how a text works" is to invite a whole range of critical procedures, including those we normally associate with the classroom. Pope begins one exercise involving "My Last Duchess" in a way that will seem mostly familiar to anyone who has taught an introductory literature course:

As you read, ask yourself:
1. how far you personally are prepared to adopt the Duke's position (e.g. his "voice" and self image);
2. what other position(s) you feel yourself drawn to adopt (even though they may have no "voices" or self-images directly available). (15)

Normally we think of such questions as ways to get the discussion moving—as a prelude to deeper matters involving agency, reliability, what is said, and what is not said. Pope, though, has a totally different project in mind (or, rather, and I will return to this in a moment, the same project reimagined with a new *techne*). As the exercise proceeds, students are "translating" the poem into their own conversational idiom, making *lists* of who is present and who is excluded (including the people who built the wall and the terrace, made the Duchess's mantle, and tend the orchard), and finally, rewriting the poem from a new center.

Jerome McGann and Lisa Samuels refer to such procedures as instances of "deformance"—a word that usefully combines a number of terms, including "form," "deform," and "performance." The centerpiece of their essay is a quote from Emily Dickinson: "Did you ever read one of her Poems backward, because the plunge from the front overturned you? I sometimes (often have, many times) have—a Something overtakes the Mind—" (qtd. in McGann 106). The injunction attempts a disordering of our critical apprehensions that suggests an alignment with the disorderings of Jarry. Reading a poem backward is like viewing the face of a watch sideways—a way of unleashing the potentialities that altered perspectives may reveal:

Reading backward is a critical move that invades these unvisited precincts of imaginative works. It is our paradigm of any kind of deformative critical operation.

Such a model brings to attention areas of the poetic and artifactual media that usually escape our scrutiny. But this enlargement of the subject matter of criticism doesn't define the most significant function of deformative operations. Far more important is the stochastic process it entails. Reading backward is a highly regulated method for disordering the senses of a text. It turns off the controls that organize the poetic system at some of its most general levels. When we run the deformative program through a particular work we cannot predict the results. As Dickinson elegantly put it, "A Something overtakes the Mind," and we are brought to a critical position in which we can imagine things about the text that we didn't and perhaps couldn't otherwise know. (McGann 116)

There are several reasons why these ideas, so culturally detached from the mathematical rigidity of computation, should resonate with creators of computational tools for literary study. Anyone who has marked up a text in a metalanguage for machine manipulation, tokenized strings for word-frequency analysis, or undertaken any of the dozens of allegedly pre-interpretative activities that go into designing computer systems for humanistic study has already come face-to-face with "the poetic and artifactual media that usually escape our scrutiny." Encoding texts in XML (extensible markup language) places one in a simultaneously cooperative and antagonistic relationship with the codes that already subsist in written works. Optical character-recognition software reveals the fragility of the grapheme. Tokenization forces us to confront the fact that the notion of a word is neither unambiguous nor satisfactorily definable for all circumstances. Rather than hindering the process of critical engagement, this relentless exactitude produces a critical self-consciousness that is difficult to achieve otherwise. In pouring the "well of English undefiled" through the thin opening of Von Neumann's bottleneck, we discover strange tensions, exceptions, and potentials.

Even the simplest of transformations yields insights about the nature of poetic form. Consider, for example, Emily Dickinson's invitation to "tell it slant":

> Tell all the truth but tell it slant—
> Success in Circuit lies
> Too bright for our infirm Delight
> The Truth's superb surprise
>
> As lightning to the Children eased
> With explanation kind
> The Truth must dazzle gradually
> Or every man be blind—   .
>   (506–7)

This poem puts forth a poetics, but it might also be understood as a poetical description of our own methodologies as critics. The critic implicitly considers the "Truth's superb surprise" in literature—however contingent, however distanced from notions of objectivity—as being at a slant, always behind or beneath the denotative meanings of the words involved. Untangling the Circuit, restoring it to a logical and linear pattern of meaning and deduction, constitutes one of the chief activities of criticism as such. In this sense, poetry has always demanded something like "close reading." Instead of letting words continue on (as in oral recitation), the reader pauses to consider the patterns that emerge from various combinations of textual information. Often, those patterns occur at those moments where the language seems at odds—at a slant—from normal usage: *infirm* delight, success *in circuit,* the odd semantics of "As lightning to the Children eased," the capitalizations of "Truth," "Children," "Circuit," and "Delight" (though not "explanation," "lightning," "surprise" or "blind"). The backward poem deepens this engagement by revealing other forces and tensions that the forward arrangement conceals:

> Or every man be blind—
> The Truth must dazzle gradually
> With explanation kind
> As lightning to the Children eased
>
> The Truth's superb surprise
> Too bright for our infirm Delight
> Success in Circuit lies
> Tell all the truth but tell it slant—[1]

We who have grown accustomed to intelligibility borne of close analysis may expect nonsense to emerge from this operation, but the effect (as Dickinson intuited) is quite different. Some phrases do seem strangely contorted. The first line, in fact, seems the strangest of all—as if we were coming to the poem in medias res. We are almost invited to read it as if it ended not with Dickinson's ubiquitous em-dash, but with a colon: "Here are the things we must do to avoid blindness: . . ." The next movement of the poem, though, is a complete sentence: "The Truth must dazzle gradually / With explanation kind / As lightning to the children eased." That it should so closely resemble how one might paraphrase the thought of the original serves to illuminate the very "slanting" that Dickinson imposed upon the ordinary language from which the poem draws both its strangeness and its intelligibility. The rhymes remain in both stanzas, but the inversion of ABCB to the somewhat heterodox ABAC almost renders them invisible. The poem is as iambic backward as it is forward, but without the end-rhymes, the poem slips quietly into the cadence of prose. The appositional structure of the second stanza (or, rather, the first stanza) presents itself more strongly than before. The last line, as so often happens with this particular reading strategy, seems slightly bathetic.

What had been a bold announcement of the poem's intent in the original, now seems almost like a limp punch line or a bon mot.

Irizarry's work, in what the Oulipians might gleefully call an instance of "anticipatory plagiary," enacts the principles of deformance in explicitly machinic terms. The move is inspired not by Oulipo, but by a constellation of Hispanic poets ranging from Pas and Borges to Juan-Eduardo Circlot and Clara Janés, all of whom "have examined substitution and permutation in theory and practice:"

> Computer-enabled "play" can accomplish the same type of alteration which these writers have pursued in their works. Such poetic play, beyond the poetic products themselves, serves as a tool to increase readers' awareness of poetry by a unique blend of word, structure, and pattern. By imbuing the poetic text with a new dimension, on-screen manipulation of what has been called "electric poetry" (Silverstein) evokes the reader's participation in the poetic process. The interactive modality offered by the electronic medium destabilizes the text, allowing the reader to explore it more thoroughly than is possible in the fixed printed medium and to both appreciate and experience poetry as "play." (Irizarry 155)

Irizarry thus envisions a group of what we might call "deformance machines": small programs designed to effect algorithmic transformations of poetic works.

Irizarry suggests the transformation of a lyric poem into an "entropic poem" in which all word-level redundancy has been removed. Poems that rely on repetition, however subtly, are particularly suited to this method. Here is Dylan Thomas's "The Force That through the Green Fuse Drives the Flower":

> The force that through the green fuse drives the flower
> Drives my green age; that blasts the roots of trees
> Is my destroyer.
> And I am dumb to tell the crooked rose
> My youth is bent by the same wintry fever.
>
> The force that drives the water through the rocks
> Drives my red blood; that dries the mouthing streams
> Turns mine to wax.
> And I am dumb to mouth unto my veins
> How at the mountain spring the same mouth sucks.
>
> The hand that whirls the water in the pool
> Stirs the quicksand; that ropes the blowing wind
> Hauls my shroud sail.
> And I am dumb to tell the hanging man
> How of my clay is made the hangman's lime.

The lips of time leech to the fountain head;
Love drips and gathers, but the fallen blood
Shall calm her sores.
And I am dumb to tell a weather's wind
How time has ticked a heaven round the stars.

And I am dumb to tell the lover's tomb
How at my sheet goes the same crooked worm.

(Thomas 90)

Here is the entropic version—a word-frequency list that retains the order of the words.[2]

25 the	5 dumb	1 mine	1 hauls	1 shall
2 force	7 to	1 wax	1 shroud	1 calm
6 that	4 tell	2 mouth	1 sail	1 her
2 through	2 crooked	1 unto	1 hanging	1 sores
2 green	1 rose	1 veins	1 man	2 a
1 fuse	1 youth	4 how	1 clay	1 weather's
4 drives	1 bent	2 at	1 made	1 has
1 flower	1 by	1 mountain	1 hangman's	1 ticked
8 my	3 same	1 spring	1 lime	1 heaven
1 age	1 wintry	1 sucks	1 lips	1 round
1 blasts	1 fever	1 hand	2 time	1 stars
1 roots	2 water	1 whirls	1 leech	1 lover's
3 of	1 rocks	1 in	1 fountain	1 tomb
1 trees	1 red	1 pool	1 head	1 sheet
3 is	2 blood	1 stirs	1 love	1 goes
1 destroyer	1 dries	1 quicksand	1 drips	1 worm
6 and	1 mouthing	1 ropes	1 gathers	
5 I	1 streams	1 blowing	1 but	
5 am	1 turns	2 wind	1 fallen	

The entropic poem shares a family resemblance with the output of word-frequency analysis tools, which are among the fundamental computational primitives of text analysis. Like the lists generated by such tools, the new formation enters the space of the poem as a statistical paratext. But by retaining the order of the words, the entropic poem declares itself more forcefully to be what even the most apparently disinterested word-frequency list already is: a deformation of the original. It is a readable work that maintains its coherence fully until the thinning logic of compression overtakes it.

Irizarry's use of the word "entropy" recalls the use of that term in information theory, where it signifies the degree of order in a system. In information theoretical terms, the program that generated the new formation strives to bring the poem from a state of low- to high-order entropy by reducing the number of symbols necessary to encode the information. At times, that process is quite successful, as when the algorithm produces the cryptic "water rocks red blood" for "The force that drives the water through the rocks / Drives my red blood." The algorithm suggestively fails to compress at the ends of stanzas where a certain sense reemerges: "youth bent by same wintry fever," "made hangman's lime," "fallen shall calm her sores," "ticked heaven round stars," and "lover's tomb sheet goes worm." The entropic poem does not so much provide data about the original poem as focus our attention on certain energies in the original—in this case, similar movements in thought redescribed in new terms at the ends of stanzas.

One is perhaps tempted to consider such possible tools of algorithmic criticism as mere amusements—the critical readings they engender, as hermeneutical curiosities wholly unrelated to the practices of conventional critical reading. McGann and Samuels, however, propose that "we may usefully regard all criticism and interpretation as deformance," since all interpretation represents "the application of scientia to poiesis, or the effort to elucidate one discourse form in terms of another" (127).[3] In this view, deformance becomes not just "the best way" (as in Pope), or the new way (as in Irizarry), but an extreme form of the only way—the way it has always been done.

To speak of algorithmic criticism is to take a further step and imagine this generalization as an explicit technological program for critical reading. Texts that have become proverbial among students of new media, like the Talmud and the *I Ching*, are particularly useful here. Because they are often held up as foreshadowings of the ergodic, the interactive, and the hypertextual—that is, as unusual and distinct forms of reading and writing—there has been a tendency to deemphasize their continuity with the more normative practices of reading and writing. They provide useful test cases for the idea that all criticism and interpretation is deformance.

One consults the *I Ching* in order to determine the auspiciousness or inauspiciousness of a course of action and to gain some sense of how that course is likely to unfold. With the question in mind, the reader/diviner throws three coins or yarrow stalks and arrives at a combination that will resolve to one of four numbers (six, seven, eight, or nine). Each of these numbers corresponds to one of two states for a particular line of a hexagram. If one throws a six or an eight, the line is a broken line; a seven or a nine results in a whole line. In order to determine the path and outcome of my writing on computation and literary criticism, I threw three coins six times to determine all of the lines and then stacked them on top of one another to create the following hexagram:

In this case, the figure corresponds to the twenty-first hexagram, which bears the tag *shike* ("biting"). In Richard Rutt's translation, I am led to a page with the following text:

Sacrifice.
Favourable in disputes.

Base (9):   Shackled with leg-fetters:
            mutilating the feet.
                                            NO MISFORTUNE.

(6) 2:   Biting flesh:
            mutilating the nose.
                                            NO MISFORTUNE.

(6) 3:   Biting dried meat:
            getting poison to eat.
                                        Little distress.
                                            NO MISFORTUNE.

(9) 4:   Biting ham in the rind:
            a bronze arrow to find.
                                Favourable in hardship augury.
                                        AUGURY AUSPICIOUS.

(6) 5:   Biting pemmican:
            finding golden bronze.
                                    Augury DANGEROUS.
                                            NO MISFORTUNE.

Top (9):   Shouldering a cangue:
            mutilating the ears.
                                            DISASTER.

(Rutt 244)

The specific values for each line subdivide further into stable and changeable whole and broken lines. The "stack" of solid and broken lines contain certain lines that are understood to have complements in the opposite formation (certain broken lines that correspond to whole lines, and vice versa). If the top (unbroken) line in the previous hexagram were "unstable" (a value determined by the numeric value of the coins) and all the rest were stable, we would need to find another hexagram that corresponds exactly to the previous one, but with the top line broken. The visual metaphor is roughly that of two broken lines moving toward one another to form a whole, or conversely, a whole line stretching to the point of breaking into two. We would then understand the above oracle as referring to an additional text corresponding to hexagram 17 *(sui/pursuit)*:

Supreme offering.
Favourable in disputes.

NO MISFORTUNE.

Base (9):   A building collapses.

Augury AUSPICIOUS.
Being crossed on leaving home: there will be success.

Base (9):
(6) 2:   Binding little ones, losing grown men.
(6) 3:   Binding grown men, losing little ones.

Pursuit ends in catching the quarry.
Augury for a dwelling: favourable.

(9) 4:   Pursuit ends in finding.

Augury: DISASTROUS.
Sacrificing captives on the way;
in a covenant, could there be misfortune?

(9) 5:   Captives at a triumph.

AUSPICIOUS.

Top (6):   Brought in bonds, let them be guarded.

The king offers them at the West Mountain.

(Rutt 240)

Espen Aarseth considers the *I Ching* a prime example of an ergodic cybertext—a genre that includes both Web-based hypertext and computer adventure games. Two features make it so. First, "nontrivial effort is required to allow the reader to traverse the text" (1). The mantic nature of the work demands "a highly specialized ritual of perusal" quite different from the act of turning the pages of a novel (2). Second, the *I Ching* constantly reminds the reader of "inaccessible strategies and paths not taken, voices not heard" (3).

The first requirement is clearly met in this case. One does not ordinarily read narrative works by casting lots and turning to pages by chance, but in this case the stochastic element is clearly part of the nature of the work. The second requirement is likewise fulfilled: chance dictates only one of 4,096 (64^2) possible "perusals" of the text at a given moment. We are left to wonder what a head might have revealed where a tail was cast. In both cases, however, we may suspect merely a more pronounced version of properties that obtain in any text. Aarseth anticipates these objections at the beginning of his book on ergodic literature:

> Whenever I have had the opportunity to present the perspective of ergodic literature and cybertext to a fresh audience of literary critics and theorists, I have almost invariably been challenged on the same issues: that these texts (hypertexts, adventure games, etc.) aren't essentially different from other literary texts, because (1) all literature is to some extent indeterminate, nonlinear, and different for every reading, (2) the reader has to make choices in order to make sense of the text, and finally (3) a text cannot really be nonlinear because the reader can read it only one sequence at a time, anyway. (2)

These objections suffer, as Aarseth rightly claims, from a lack of distinction and specification. That all texts might be nonlinear effaces the obvious distinctions between a text that involves yarrow stalks and one that does not; that no text can be nonlinear reduces cognition to temporality. Aarseth's response to these objections, however, underestimates the haptic nature of the critical act:

> A reader, however strongly engaged in the unfolding of a narrative, is powerless. Like a spectator at a soccer game, he may speculate, conjecture, extrapolate, even shout abuse, but he is not a player. Like a passenger on a train, he can study and interpret the shifting landscape, he may rest his eyes wherever he pleases, even release the emergency brake and step off, but he is not free to move the tracks in a different direction. He cannot have the player's pleasure or influence: "Let's see what happens when I do this." The reader's pleasure is the pleasure of the voyeur. Safe, but impotent. (4)

The minute someone proposes to explain the meaning of a narrative—to speculate, conjecture, extrapolate, or shout abuse at it, whether in the privacy of one's thoughts or in a critical journal—the narrative changes, because we are no longer able to read it without knowledge of the paratextual revolt.

Chinua Achebe's charges of racism in Joseph Conrad's *Heart of Darkness* is a case in point. By remapping the resonances of the characters and events in that narrative, Achebe alters that narrative by literally adding text to the document space of the novel. Achebe locates passages in which Africans are represented and counts the instances in which Conrad has the characters speak (twice: once to express a desire to eat a white man, and a second to say "Mistah Kurtz—he dead") (Achebe 9). He gathers other writings by Conrad, including an appalling account of his first encounter with a "buck nigger" and the "blind, furious, unreasoning rage" it evoked in him ever after (13). The opinions of other critics are cited, including the (still prevalent) idea that Africa "is merely the setting for the disintegration of the mind of Mr. Kurtz" (12). All of these procedures—quotation, summary, paraphrase, conjecture— come precisely as a result of having said, "Let's see what happens when I do *this*"; the "this" is a rewritten *Heart of Darkness*.

Such representations are hardly impotent. The consequences of a *Heart of Darkness* rewritten so as to expose its racism will have the tangible effect of limiting (and in some cases, destroying) many of the other narrative possibilities with which it is inextricably linked. It may even have the result of ensuring that this narrative, which Achebe calls "offensive and deplorable," is dropped from course syllabi—in effect guaranteeing that certain types of transformations are never undertaken again (14). Aarseth continues:

> The effort and energy demanded by the cybertext of its reader raise the stakes of interpretation to those of intervention. Trying to know a cybertext is an investment of personal improvisation that can result in either intimacy or failure. The tensions at work in a cybertext, while not incompatible with those of narrative desire, are also something more: a struggle not merely for interpretative insight but also for narrative control: "I want this text to tell my story; the story could not be without me." In some cases this is literally true. (4)

But again, is it not literally true whenever anyone tries to explain what a narrative means (such explanations being the only tangible evidence we have of a reading experience)? In Achebe's article this desire to make the text tell a different story is palpably evident, since he proposes that *Heart of Darkness* does not tell his story and must now be made to do so. Achebe's story does not metaphorically intervene in this case; it literally intervenes—reinscribing the words of the text of the book itself—in order to demonstrate that the narrative of *Heart of Darkness* "cannot be" without his story. Terms like "intervention" and "struggle for narrative control" describe perfectly those interpretative actions (which is to say, all interpretative actions) that create an alternative version of the text itself.

The interest that the *I Ching* holds for the student of new (or old) media lies in the singularity of form that these narrative interventions and struggles for control assume, not in the fact that one may (as with any text) intervene and attempt to control its meaning. Throwing coins to choose texts, while an interesting and essential feature of this particular text, remains one of the least significant elements in terms of one's ability to engage in these practices. One narrative possibility of the *I Ching*—one that attempts to make the book tell my story—understands the passage of hexagram 21 to 17 as relating directly to the writing of this book. The idea for this work came in the midst of other work. Pursuing this project therefore meant "sacrificing" work to which I felt metaphorically "shackled." Before undertaking the project, I exchanged a series of e-mails with a colleague in which we "disputed" the viability of the topic—disputes that nonetheless had the "favorable" result of convincing me to pursue the work. Once I set myself to the task of explicating the relationship between computer analysis of texts and literary critical practice, I found that I had to "bite through" a series of difficult articulations punctuated with what seemed like "pointed" problems I was discussing (the "bronze arrow" and "golden bronze" of the line statements). At one point I managed to erase the file I was working on (unmistakably prophesied in the final prognostic: "DISASTER"). Hexagram 17 presumably forecasts the successful conclusion of the work, which, considering the lessons learned from having once erased the file, will indeed be "guarded" when it is "brought in bounds" to the printer.

This is not essentially different from saying that Tennyson's "In Memoriam" speaks to me or that Sartre's *Les Mots* is the story of my life. Nor is it fundamentally different from saying that the former draws upon contemporary accounts of geological and evolutionary time, or that the latter is most successfully elucidated with reference to Heidegger. Here I am re-presenting the text so that it speaks literally about my life.[4] The source of this knowledge comes either from my own inventiveness (or perversity) as a reader, or from the fact that the mantic qualities of the text are literally true. In either case—in all cases—I am presenting a new text that imputes or denies authority to the original text itself, legitimizing or de-legitimizing its claims to truth value, proclaiming its power to mean or demonstrating my own power to do the same.

The power dynamics of the alternative text are equally visible in the hands of eighteenth-century Jesuit missionaries eager to demonstrate the ways in which the ancient Chinese classics might be adapted to Christianity. Jean-François Foucquet, despite papal condemnation of such "accommodationist" strategies, tried to show how the *I Ching* parallels the Old Testament (Rutt 63). Hexagram 13, for example, became a text about the Fall of Man (here quoted in James Legge's 1882 translation):

Thung Zăn (or "Union of men") appears here (as we find it) in the (remote districts of the) country, indicating progress and success. It will be advantageous to cross the great stream. It will be advantageous to maintain the firm correctness of the superior man.

1. The first NINE, undivided, (shows the representative of) the union of men just issuing from his gate. There will be no error.
2. The second SIX, divided, (shows the representative of) the union of men in relation with his kindred. There will be occasion for regret.
3. The third NINE, undivided, (shows its subject) with his arms hidden in the thick grass, and at the top of a high mound. (But) for three years he makes no demonstration.
4. The fourth NINE, undivided, (shows its subject) mounted on the city wall; but he does not proceed to make the attack (he contemplates). There will be good fortune.
5. In the fifth NINE undivided, (the representative of) the union of men first wails and cries out, then laughs. His great host conquers, and he (and the subject of the second line) meet together.
6. The topmost NINE, undivided, (shows the representative of) the union of men in the suburbs. There will be no occasion of repentance. (86–87)

If we read the hexagram within this rubric, the message seems clear. But to read within a rubric is precisely to impose a set of procedures upon a text. In this case the motives for those procedures are religious and political. The English Bible and the *I Ching* cross-fertilize each other in such a way as to bring "the superior man," "men just issuing from his gate," "men in relation to his kindred," and "There will be no occasion of repentance" to the forefront of our attention. Phrases like "arms hidden in the thick grass" and "the union of men in the suburbs," though perhaps eminently meaningful to a feudal ruler about to wage war, recede into the background of our attention.

Even in the case of the *I Ching*, we can see examples of reading practices that strongly resemble Achebe's attempt to alter the permissible meanings of that text. The Song philosopher Shao Yong discovered a coherent mathematical order to the hexagrams, which was then presumed to be the original order. So effective was his attempt at authorization that it would later come to be known as the *Xiantin*—the "earlier than heaven" sequence (Rutt 90). More famous still are the reformations undertaken by Confucians of the late Han dynasty, who, in an effort to validate the great classic for Confucian scholars (no doubt hesitant, given Confucius's legendary opposition to divination), came to associate the text with the golden age of Confucianism during the Zhou period. Eventually the story came to be told that Confucius himself admired the *I Ching*:

> This idea, which was current for a thousand years, depended on a single sentence in the Analects, the collection of sayings that is our only source for Confucius's teaching. In Legge's translation of Analects vii. 16, this sentence reads: "If some years were added to my life, I would give fifty to the study of the *Yi*, and then I might come to be without great faults." The Lu text of the Analects, now preferred by most scholars, has the word *yi* written with another character of the same sound, meaning not "change," but "also" or "more." This makes the sentence mean: "If I were given a few more years, so that I might spend a whole fifty in study, I believe that after all I should be fairly free from error." (Rutt 33)

Rutt notes, "This is likely the correct reading"—and it may be, in the technical sense—but it must be pointed out that this scholarly reading constitutes yet another attempt to reform the potential textualities of the text.

In most cases the creation of alternative textualities serves the ordinary purpose of allowing us to generate meaning from what we read. The patterns we generate—summaries and paraphrases, for example—serve precisely to select a narrow set of meanings from the field of all possible meanings. We may create this set either in opposition to or in cooperation with the rhetorics that we perceive the text itself putting forth. The *I Ching* is notable not for allowing this behavior, but for the way in which it generates a worldview from the consequences of this behavior. Whatever one might consider the specific contours of that worldview to be, it is a worldview (or perhaps a text view) liberated from the suspicion that subjectivity compromises meaning. We cannot avoid finding meaning in the *I Ching*, because our history, our circumstances, our desires, and our anxieties—indeed, the entire constellation of subjective interests we possess—form the inescapable precondition upon which the intelligibility of the text depends. Admirers of the *I Ching* have for centuries recognized the wisdom of this engagement. There is, of course, nothing in the text itself to contradict them.

Both the *I Ching* and the work of the Oulipo call attention to the always dissolving boundaries between creation and interpretation. Despite this, both productions are ordinarily considered aesthetic in nature and thus impervious to the objections often leveled against more overtly interpretative works. The agonistic relationship between artistic deformation and critical legitimacy are far more evident when a work declares itself as primarily interpretative, and nowhere is this anxiety more poignant than in Ferdinand de Saussure's research on pre-classical Latin poetry, the details of which form the subject of a number of unpublished notebooks written between 1906 and 1909.

The Greek-influenced quantitative meters of golden-age Latin—the poetry of Horace, Catullus, and Martial—were ordered according to a well-understood set of rules governing vowel length. The formal guidelines of pre-classical "Saturnian" verse, however, are quite a bit more difficult to discern. Much of the poetry is characterized by assonance, alliteration, and parallelism structured in such a way as to suggest a pattern, but students of Latin poetry have for centuries differed over how to state that pattern programmatically, even debating whether the form is accentual or metrical in nature.

Saussure begins his attempt at solving the "problem" of Saturnian poetry by focusing on those elements that seem clearly part of the prosodic architecture of the verse: assonance and alliteration. But Saussure's breakthrough comes from a change of focus not at all unlike the decision to read a poem backward or to impose Oulipian constraints upon it. Saussure sees the phonemes in isolation, unmoored from the wider denotative meaning of the poem, and begins to count them. He soon discovers that while the pattern of syllabification in a Saturnian poem varies, the number of consonants and vowels in each line occurs according to a subtle but unmistakably patterned regularity. Put simply, most of the vowels and consonants in each line have an accompanying "counter" or repeated term. Those vowels and consonants that do not have a counter produce a modulo character that is then carried over onto the next line. Saussure deduced that the poet must be trying to fit the verse into a pattern of even-numbered alliterations. Failing that, the extra consonant or vowel would "overflow" to the next verse unit. "The result is so startling that one wonders how the authors of these lines . . . would have found the time for such onerous and minute calculation: for Saturnian verse, quite apart from any metric considerations, is like a Chinese game in its complexity" (Saussure, qtd. in Starobinsky 9).

That complexity, brought forth by the decision to see a poem in a way utterly counter to what we would normally consider reading, soon yields further patterns. Before long, Saussure is beginning to notice graphic and phonemic patterns that are themselves suggestive of a much deeper order. Considered in isolation, the common phonemes and the unpaired consonants begin to re(as)semble independent words, which, Saussure concludes, must form the "theme word" from which the rest of the poem is formed:

> Thus, if, for instance, we take as our THEME or TITLE (which is practically the same thing) Diis Manibus Luci Corneli Scipionis Sacrum, it will be necessary for the verse section of the inscription to leave free and unpaired, that is to say, in a number whose total is ODD, the letters D.M.L.C.S. |R.|
>
> Specifically, we have the first four letters because for proper names, and for consecrated formulas like Diis Manibus, it is only the INITIAL which counts. The last is R because *Sacrum,* conversely, must be taken with all its letters. But neither the S nor the C nor the M of *Sacrum* can be expressed because these letters already exist in D.M.L.C.S.—and if one added a new S or C or M to the verse section, all these letters would find themselves canceled by the even number. (13)

Saussure also comes upon phonemes that recapitulate the vowel structures of the theme word, and that further cluster around particular sets of words between the initial and final character of the theme. These clusters he calls "mannequins." If the theme word is "Aphrodite," one will find mannequins like "Amnīs ită captă lepōrE" and "Ac montīs fluviosqvE" (63–65). In one of the more extraordinary examples of this phenomenon, Saussure finds amid Lucretius's invectives against the madness of sexual passion in *De Rerum Natura,* the word "postscenia" (backstage). As Starobinsky observed, "The word which distributes its phonic elements through the text of the poem is that in which, metaphorically, a depth of artifice, a place devoid of majesty, ruled by illusion, is denounced" (74).

Saussure modifies his thesis slightly throughout the notebooks. In attempting to name the phenomenon, he suggests not only "anagram" but also "hypogram," "anaphone," "paragram," "paramine," "paronym," "paranomase," "logogram," and even "antigram." But by whatever combination of Greek roots, the essential features of the phenomenon remain the same. In dozens of examples Saussure finds an encrypted message running alongside, over, and against the aural and graphic elements of the text. If one needs to consider the phonemic and graphic elements of the text differently in light of the anagrams, then this, according to Saussure, simply demonstrates that our conception of Latin phonology is flawed:

1. Every *u* for *o* must be assumed (in 397) to be in the condition of *o*. (But still, perhaps some internal *u*'s for *o*?)
2. Every *u* for *oi* is still *oi*. And of course, *u* for *ou* is *ou*.
3. Every *i* for *ei* is still *ei,* and the only question would be if, in turn, *ei* originating in the final *oi* were not kept as *oi*. I myself generally accept *ei,* and the anagrams seem to require it. (48)

Before long, Saussure is finding anagrams not only throughout the Saturnian corpus but also in golden-age Latin, Homeric Greek, and even in Latin prose.

Saussure was well aware of the questions his findings proposed. If it is true that anagrams appear according to a thoroughly logical and discernible pattern throughout a significant portion of Latin verse, then what accounts for this pattern? Was it simply a method of composition well known to antiquity but that has failed to materialize in any of the *ars poetica* that have survived? Or do anagrams "emanate" in some way from poetical language behavior—a sort of verbal subconscious lying beneath the apparent text? Or is it merely the case that any significant sample of text will yield anagrams (particularly when the interpreter is committed to finding them)?

Such questions seem so natural to us that we tend to overlook the obvious similarities between Saussure's apparently eccentric inquiries and the more ordinary act of literary-critical interpretation. Literary-critical insight begins with a change of vision—what Wittgenstein called the "dawning of an aspect" (*Philosophical* 194). Sometimes that experience is sudden and slightly mysterious, as when one notices a pun only after several readings of a passage or sees a connection between a passage of text in one book and a passage in another; at other times (in literary criticism, one should say most other times) the noticing is the result of some sort of overt manipulation of the text. We read out of order, we translate and paraphrase, we look only at certain words or certain constellations of surrounding context. The text hasn't changed its graphic content any more than the duck-rabbit changes between one's seeing it one way one moment and another the next. But the text quite literally assumes a different organization from what it had before. Once a new aspect/pattern has been discovered, one immediately begins to test the viability of that pattern. How often does it appear? How generally does it apply? Further alteration of the text is unavoidable at this stage. In the passage quoted above, Saussure both alters his text to meet his pattern ("Every *u* for *o* must be assumed to be in the condition of *o*") and alters his sense of pattern in light of the text ("the anagrams seem to require it"). Like any literary critic, Saussure deforms and reforms his text, revealing unknown aspects of its ontology—literally creating it anew.

The risks of deformation are of a piece with the dangers of rhetoric itself. "In short, we can see outlined here the risks of an illusion—risks of which Saussure was fully aware and for which a formula might be expressed in this way: every complex structure furnishes an observer with a range of elements which will allow for him to choose a sub-ensemble apparently endowed with sense, and for which nothing prohibits *a priori* a logical or chronological antecedent" (Starobinsky 44). In one sense, deformation is the only rational response to complexity. Nearly all deformative procedures (which include outline, paraphrase, translation, and even genre description) are intended to alleviate some difficulty, in the same way that Dickinson's procedure is presented as if it were the cure to an ailment. All textual entities allow for deformation, and given that interpretation occurs amid a textual field that is by nature complex, polysemic, and multi-referential, one might say that most entities require it. Seen in this light, deformation is simply a part of our permanent capacity for sense-making. But what if, as Starobinsky suggests, *nothing prohibits* that sense-making? Is not the entire notion of "sense" called into question if complex structures will always lead to the discovery of patterns that we can then call meaningful? It is precisely this fear of an eviscerated objectivity that gives rise to those rhetorical structures that work to conceal the deformations that lie between text and interpretation. Critical discourse traditionally demands that patterns correspond to the content of the author's consciousness, or resonate in some way with sociohistorical "facts," or simply occur with enough frequency to merit naming. Anything else is open to the charge of being deemed either nonsensical or too aimless to qualify as critically coherent.

Saussure considers a number of possible explanations for the anagram. Perhaps the anagram is essentially hieratic in nature. Perhaps the frequent 4–3–3-3 blocks of syllables were originally magical formulas, or prayers, or perhaps hymns or funerary verses that contain the name of a god or other sacred word out of deference to the deity (or out of necessity for the spell) (Starobinsky 41). Survival of the form, then, would not be the secret passing on of some sort of occult knowledge, but simply that familiar linguistic/anthropological phenomenon wherein the form of a religious ritual survives long after the initial context has vanished. The absolute silence of the ancients on the subject of anagrams would therefore seem to indicate either a subject of extreme secrecy or a formalism too commonplace to require elucidation. Perhaps the anagram is merely the natural outcome of an ordinary aesthetic process. Beginning with the anagram, one notices a series of sounds and decides to work them into the verse, or the verse yields a series of sounds that one recognizes anagrammatically, and thus continues the pattern throughout.

Saussure considers the various objections at length. The question seems unresolvable from a historical standpoint; the ancients leave us with no reference to the practice whatsoever. Statistical analysis seems likewise futile. Too few anagrams in too few poems is as damaging to the validity of the theory as too many anagrams in too many poems. But in the end Saussure remains certain that his inquiries bear witness to some sort of truth:

> The "rules" representing so many accumulated powers seem to tip the balance in favor of accepting that anagrams are illusory. I respond to that with a certain confidence, committing myself to the future: A time will come when many more rules will be added to those we already have, in which the present stock of rules will appear to be simply the skeleton or framework of the complete structure. One will, on the other hand, have had time—since at present we have only taken up the most basic elements—to appreciate that the hypogram in itself is so incontestable that there is not need for anxiety, either about its actual existence or its precision, because of the many possibilities available for its various realizations. (Starobinsky 102)

One wonders, given the nature of deformative activity, whether any critical act could ever be considered "incontestable," or if, given the rubric of objectivity, the movement from text to interpretation could ever be free of anxiety.

Saussure's inquiries into anagrams, written just prior to his famous lectures on linguistics, were never published. Apart from a few carefully worded letters, he appears to have kept his research to himself. Without proof—and proof meant conscious deliberation on the part of an author—he couldn't bring himself to announce the anagram as having critical value.

> As his study of hypograms progressed, Ferdinand de Saussure showed himself capable of finding an increasing quantity of names hidden beneath a line of poetry.... But if this approach had been further developed, it would soon have become a quagmire. Wave upon wave of possible names would have taken shape beneath his alert and disciplined eye. Is this the vertigo of error? It is also the discovery of the simple truth that language is an infinite resource, and that behind each phrase lies hidden the multiple clamor from which it has detached itself to appear before us in its isolated individuality. (Starobinsky 122)

The "multiple clamor" is nothing less than the text's status as a work already deformed, already mediated by the accumulated experience of language that produced it and that the reader must have in order to read it. It lies "hidden" only if we believe that the new organizations that arise from deformative activity are revelatory of something inherent in the text before the act of interpretation. For Saussure, there was no satisfactory argument to be made for this preexistence, no line to be drawn between the deformative act and interpretative illumination. Sometime in the spring of 1909, Saussure's studies of anagrams cease.

Saussure's anxieties are rooted in a basic assumption about text and meaning. Statements of methodology, generalizations about literary significance, surmises concerning authorial intention, and various other forms of literary-theoretical philosophizing about these engagements all give the appearance of existing outside or somehow above the textuality of the object under discussion; even when we speak of meaning as "in" or arising "from" the text, we nonetheless proceed as if the meanings we generate and the texts themselves were separate entities. This same belief does not obtain for algorithmic procedures, which, because they explicitly deform their originals, tread upon the rhetorically maintained separation between text and reading. Reading strategies based substantially upon such procedures, like the ancient practice of *gematria*, the anti-art poetics of the Dadaists, the backward reading of Dickinson, and the "random" textuality of the *I Ching*, lie entirely outside the reading strategies licensed by contemporary literary-critical practice. They may constitute clever forms of amusement, anarchic forms of literary protest, vehicles for religious insight, and perhaps even objects of serious anthropological study, but not serious literary criticism itself. Yet the generation of literary-critical readings (as distinct from the more general activity of interpretation in ordinary language behavior) depends precisely upon such deformative procedures as that which Dickinson and Saussure suggest. To read a poem *as* postcolonial artifact, *as* evidence of generic protest, *as* cultural touchstone (the preposition in each case signaling the onset of deformation) is to present a narrative that depends upon a number of discrete (de)formal procedures. These procedures have the effect of creating alternative texts that form the basis of further elucidations.

This principle is amply demonstrated on page eight of the nearly two-thousand-page *Norton Anthology of Poetry.* There, students encounter a footnote to the Anglo-Saxon poem commonly referred to as "The Wife's Lament" that neatly captures the wonderfully beguiling duplicities upon which criticism depends, while at the same time echoing the combinatorial logic of the *I Ching,* the potentiality of Oulipian forms, and the anxious methodology of Saussure:

> This poem appears in the Exeter Book, a tenth-century manuscript collection of Old English poetry, immediately following a series of riddles. Different translations offer somewhat different interpretations of the poem; the one below suggests that the poem is a dramatic monologue spoken by a wife separated from her husband. Some critics have suggested that the poem may be an allegory in which the speaker represents either the soul or the children of Israel during the Babylonian captivity. (Ferguson, Salter, and Stallworthy 8)

The idea that a poem might have an apparent meaning in addition to other analogical and typological meanings constitutes one of the core principles of criticism as such, with a tradition stretching back to the biblical hermeneutics of the Patristic age. Spatial metaphors suggest themselves, and our students intuitively echo the language of biblical exegetes by speaking of this doubleness in terms of meaning and "deeper" meaning. This footnote, however, subtly indicates that the doubleness here is more than usually problematic, since the editors felt compelled to note the obvious fact that different translations yield different interpretations. In fact, the "correct" interpretation of "The Wife's Lament" is one of the more hotly debated subjects in medieval studies.

The critic Jerome Mandel, in a book that goes by the magnificent title *Alternative Readings in Old English Poetry,* suggests that the poem "suffers from too many interpretations":

> The speaker of the poem, the "I," may be either a man or a woman who is either young or old. His or her lord or husband (1) is exiled as a result of a feud, (2) goes into exile voluntarily, (3) goes on a military expedition, (4) goes on a journey over the sea, or (5) is forced into exile by kinsmen who hate him or by revolutionary forces for political reasons. Either he returns or he does not

return. The wife is maligned to her husband or to another lord (from whom she has sought protection) for marital unfaithfulness, witchcraft, plotting against him, or some other crime. She is exiled once or twice, voluntarily or by force, into her own (or her husband's) land or into a foreign land. He banishes her because he has been tricked or he has not been tricked. She looks upon him as cruel for banishing her or for plotting some evil (perhaps murder) against her; or she looks upon him as sympathetic to her, an unwilling dupe of his kinsmen. Either she bewails her husband's altered mood (his hatred of her) or reveals her unqualified pity and respect for him who is guiltless and victimized. Or, if there are two lords, one may be cruel and one sympathetic to her. She must endure his hatred of her, or she must suffer for the hatred (probably the result of a feud) that others direct at her lord, or she must suffer persecution by the world in general. Her place of banishment or captivity is an *eorðscrafu* which is either (1) a ruin overgrown with briars, (2) a grove-dwelling, (3) a cave, (4) a succession of chambers as in natural caves, (5) a heathenish abode, (6) a prison, (7) some sort of sanctuary or monastery or nunnery, (8) an old and neglected but fortified building, (9) pit-houses or sunken huts, or (10) the grave (cf. The Wanderer 84). The poem closes with either a cry of despair, a prediction of trouble for her husband, gnomic verses suggested by reflection on her husband (or herself, or himself), an exhortation, or a curse directed either at her husband or at a third person (perhaps one of the mischievous relatives) who has come between them. (149–50)

The existence of so many competing, perhaps incommensurable readings of a work of literature is part of the normal course of literary studies. Mandel's extraordinary literature review, satirical yet clearly the result of a certain sense of frustration, captures well the ways in which minor alterations in a text—subtle changes of perspective and emphasis—metastasize throughout an interpretation. The paragraph almost resembles the control structures of modern programming languages: *if* x is true, *then* y is also true, or *else* we must default to a different set of variables or pursue a different procedure. The combinatorics of the interpretative field have elicited at least one plea of nolo contendere on the part of a critic, who, in a footnote to an article subtitled "'The Wife's Lament' as Riddle," stated, "No translation of the entire poem has been provided because any translation is tendentious, including mine" (Walker-Pelkey 242).

Mandel's own transformation of the poem begins with the simplest of procedures: he interprets (which is to say, substitutes) the "Ic" of the poem as referring to a man, thus rejecting the idea that the feminine endings of *geomorre, minre,* and *sylfre* ("sorrowful," "my," and "self" respectively) in the opening lines of the poem prove that the speaker is a woman. This change in perspective—ultimately, and most importantly, a graphic change that will be reinscribed into his article—radically alters the basic narrative of the poem. R. F. Leslie, an older critic often cited in the critical literature surrounding the poem, had called "The Wife's Lament" "one of the few poems in Old English literature dealing with the relationship between a man and a woman, and the only comprehensive study of a woman's thoughts and feelings"—a reading explicitly grounded in "the feminine forms in the opening lines" (3).

Interpreting the "Ic" as a woman allows certain forms of resolution by relating thematic aspects of the poem, but it complicates other aspects. The chronology of the events related in the poem seems particularly problematic when one follows through Mandel's exposition of the "ors" that radiate from that decision. This is where the rhetorical motives of criticism that seek to conceal deformative procedures are most evident:

> Most critics search for some order in the sequence of events which, they say, are presented incoherently because the speaker is a distraught woman. The lack of strict chronology reflects the poet's "attempt to portray excited feelings" (Chadwyk 31); or "the breaks in continuity are completely consistent with the ebb and flow of a woman's feelings" (Leslie 3); or "The intense emotion of the wife and the rather unsystematic organization of the poem in general indicates that the wife's hasty summary of antecedent action may be confused and unchronological" (Ward 27 [. . .]). (Mandel 150)

Mandel's paraphrase of the poem is completely counter to the one suggested in the footnote in the *Norton Anthology*. Instead of a wife who, having been placed in an "earth-cave" (*eorðscræfe*) by her husband's kinsmen, pines for her exiled husband, the poem becomes a lament by a man who, having been placed in "earth-caves" (*eorðscrafu*) by his lord's kinsmen, laments the tragedy of his situation. Just as a single grammatical assumption sets off this paraphrase, so the paraphrase alters the grammatical understanding of the most contested lines in the poem: the identity of the *geong mon* in line 42, the reading of the two *sy* clauses (lines 45–46), and the grammatical meaning of *þæt*, which governs the main clauses of the presumably gnomic end of the poem. Once again, the interpretation calls for a graphical reordering of the poem itself:

> I want to offer a new reading of these lines based upon the premise that the speaker is a thane separated from his lord. It involves identifying the geong mon (42a) as any indefinite young man with specific reference to the speaker of the poem. It also involves re-punctuating the sy-clauses. Heretofore, (1) *sinsorgna gedreag* (45a) has most often been read a variation of *breostceare* (44b); (2) *eol his worulde wyn* (46a) has been read as the subject of *sy* in l. 45b; and (3) the subject of *sy* in l. 46b has been the understood subject "he." Thus,

taking *sy* as optative, the *sy* clauses become a malediction: may all his worldly joy be dependent upon himself, may [he] be banished into a distant land" (168).

The *Norton Anthology* has this same line as "All earthly joy / Must come from his own self. Since my dear lord / Is outcast, far off in a distant land" (9).[5]

"The Wife's Lament" is the sum of its transformations from one text-space to another. It began (we presume) as a shifting set of sonic events, was inscribed onto the pages of a vellum manuscript, was transcribed into a diverse set of printed character formations, was translated into modern English, and now stands reconstructed in dozens of critical studies where it is commonly referred to by a title that does not appear in any manuscript. We might conclude that "The Wife's Lament" is a testimony to the poststructuralist insight that textuality is a shifting pattern of signification incapable of coalescing into any stable textual identity. We would do better to conclude that "The Wife's Lament" is a work that is always coalescing into stability by virtue of the readerly process of deformation.

Mandel's unusual candor as a deformative reader is perhaps licensed by the ambiguities—errors in transcription and transmission, for example—that naturally inhere in a medieval poem of uncertain provenance. But that is not to say that such operations are any less prevalent in readings of a less technical nature. Consider, for example, how Eve Kosofsky Sedgwick summarizes her now-famous argument concerning the dynamics of male homosocial desire in the English novel:

> The subject of this book is a relatively short, recent, and accessible passage of English culture, chiefly embodied in the mid-eighteenth- to mid-nineteenth-century novel. The attraction of the period to theorists of many disciplines is obvious: condensed, self-reflective, and widely influential change in economic, ideological, and gender arrangements. I will be arguing that concomitant changes in the structure of the continuum of male "homosocial desire" were tightly, often causally bound up with the other more visible changes; that the emerging pattern of male friendship, mentorship, entitlement, rivalry, and hetero- and homosexuality was in an intimate and shifting relation to class; and that no element of that pattern can be understood outside of its relation to women and the gender system as a whole. (1)

This passage presents general conclusions on the part of the author and holds out the promise of a generalized understanding for the reader. Such guarantees represent the most common way we communicate literary-critical understanding; rhetorically, the passage has the effect of letting us know that Sedgwick's interpretation of gender dynamics will serve to elucidate the eighteenth- and nineteenth-century novel. Yet one can easily trace the lineaments of deformative analysis that led to her conclusions. Male homosocial desire is a "structure," a "continuum," and a "system"—a field of "patterns" and "relations" that she will soon make "visible" to us. Sedgwick's book is ostensibly about the English novel, but it is more fundamentally a presentation of these structures and patterns. Her reading, in fact, depends upon one of the most famous patterns in literary study: "The graphic schema on which I am going to be drawing most heavily in the readings that follow is the triangle. The triangle is useful as a figure by which the 'commonsense' of our intellectual tradition schematizes erotic relations, and because it allows us to condense into a juxtaposition with that folk-perception several somewhat different streams of recent thought" (21). The triangle indeed functions not as an algorithm, but as something more basic: a pattern transducer—a machine for mapping one symbol set onto another. Rhetorically, it asks, "Have you ever read one of Shakespeare's sonnets as a triangle?"

Sedgwick uses this particular pattern transducer to read Shakespeare's sonnets in a way that is both trenchant and novel. She begins by acknowledging the "notorious mysteries" that seem to set the poems (and their readers) free from any stable extratextual environment: "whether they are a sequence, when they were written, to whom and to how many people addressed, how autobiographical, how conventional, why published, etc." (29). The interpretation relies upon an assumption that this absence helps to enable—namely, that the sonnets form "a continuous erotic narrative" played out among "the poet, a fair youth, a rival poet, and a dark lady" (29). Armed with the notion of a triangulation between erotic antagonists, Sedgwick is able to transform this perception of general pattern into a vision of these poems as erotic negotiations between men.

Sedgwick's graphical maneuver explicitly deforms the poem from one state to another. As an instance of language behavior, such alternate formations constitute the common currency of literary-critical (and much general human communicative) behavior. If one were to ask Sedgwick, "What does Sonnet 42 mean?" and she responded by repeating the poem, we would be within our rights to wonder if she understood what "meaning" was. To ask for an interpretation is to ask for more—and different—words. To present the poem as a triangle, to suggest that such triangles may lie elsewhere, and to use the triangle as a means for clarifying and elucidating the hidden, nondominant motives of a text is to deform with a purpose.

It is precisely the absence of this detail that renders Dickinson's suggestion (and the algorithmic criticism from which it descends) so strange. The apparent randomness with which she suggests the procedure and the implicit faith in that "Something" that will overtake the mind deliberately eschews those rhetorical procedures that seek to conceal the status of a text as alternative. For a critical argument to succeed, it must present its alternative text as a legitimate counterpart—even a consequence—of the original. Sedgwick can re-form Sonnet 144 into

love #1	love #2
comfort	despair
better	worser
MAN	WOMAN
right fair	coloured ill
angel	devil
purity	foul pride
angel	fiend
from me #1	from me #2
friend #1	friend #2
. . .	. . .

(30)

because we are on the way to a justification for why the alternative text elucidates the original:

> The basic configuration here, then, includes a stylized female who functions as a subject of action but not of thought; a stylized male who functions as pure object; and a less stylized male speaker who functions as a subject of thought but not of action. Uncommonsensical as it may be, this conformation is very characteristic of the Sonnets as a whole, and is recurrent in the plays. What interests me here is not the devastating thoroughness with which the Sonnets record and thematize misogyny and gynephobia, but rather the ways in which that plays off against the range of male bonds and speaker's programmatic assertions of symmetry. (33)

Sedgwick's deformation is indeed "uncommonsensical," but as she herself acknowledges, that deformation has led to a "conformation" now made visible throughout Shakespeare's work.

By one definition of the term, "deformation" suggests nothing more than the basic textual maneuvers by which form gives way to form—the "de" functioning not as a privative, but as relatively straightforward signifier of change. But any reading that undertakes such changes (as all reading must) remains threatened with the possibility that deformation signals loss, corruption, and illegitimacy. Even now, in our poststructuralist age, we speak of "faithfulness" to a text, of "flawed" or "misguided" readings, but any marking of a text, any statement that is not a re-performance of a statement, must break faith with the ability of the text to mean and re-guide form into alternative intelligibilities.

Algorithmic criticism is, in this sense, nothing more than a self-conscious attempt to place such re-performances into a computational environment. But within this move there lies a fundamental remonstration against our anxiety about the relationship between text and reading. Those activities that are usually seen as anathema to the essential goal of literary criticism—quantitative analysis chief among them—will need to be reconsidered if it turns out that backward poems lie at the root of our forward endeavors. Our fear of breaking faith with the text may also need to give way to a renewed faith in the capacity of subjective engagement for liberating the potentialities of meaning.

4 THE TURING TEXT

Even scholars working far outside the disciplines that make up the field of artificial intelligence are familiar with the basic elements of the Turing test, in which the machine's ability to mimic human language is presented as the touchstone of intelligent behavior. It is usually presented in the following way: A human being and an entity that is either a human being or a machine are separated from each other by a wall. The first human is allowed to pose questions to the unseen entity by means of a teleprompter. If that human being is unable to determine from the responses given whether the entity on the other side is a machine or a human being, that entity is for all intents and purposes intelligent.[1]

Turing's thought experiment has led to innumerable meditations on the possibilities for intelligent machines. But at the heart of the Turing test lies a brilliant, if unsuccessful, attempt to move attention away from the "how" of imperative process toward the results of rhetorical persuasion. Rather than having humans compete against machines in their ability to generate correct utterances, the test sets the machine's ability to generate intelligibility against the human's capacity to generate theories by which the origins and form of that intelligibility may be explained. Even if it fails to persuade (and many have suggested that the test is too easy), it fails in an entirely spectacular way. Our attention becomes focused not merely on whether its utterances are true, but on whether its utterances are possible. The "text" of the test is one in which we move from the already potentialized valences of dialogue to ruminations about the origins of that dialogue.

That one can move fruitfully between these two registers is amply, if ironically, illustrated in the case of Joseph Weizenbaum's 1960 program ELIZA, which imitates (Weizenbaum would say "parodies") the behavior of a Rogerian psychiatrist:[2]

> ELIZA: Hello, I am a computer program.
> YOU: Are you?
> ELIZA: You're not really talking about me—are you?
> YOU: Can you help me?
> ELIZA: Does someone else believe I help you?
> YOU: I'm thinking you might be able to help me!
> ELIZA: Do you wish to believe I might be able to help you?
> YOU: Yes.
> ELIZA: Please go on.
> YOU: I'm concerned about my computer.
> ELIZA: What do you think about machines?
> YOU: I think machines can be very useful for scholars.
> ELIZA: Why do you mention computers?
> YOU: I don't know.
> ELIZA: Don't you really know? (*Chatbot::ELIZA*)

Weizenbaum made no pretensions toward setting aside the "how" of his program. Behind ELIZA's dialogue lies a fairly rudimentary keyword substitution algorithm that mostly parrots back the user's responses (while trying to avoid repetition). The effect, though, is legendary. There are several anecdotes (some undoubtedly apocryphal, all plausible), in which ELIZA tricks someone's employer or colleague into thinking that ELIZA is a real person, and Weizenbaum himself observed (to his horror and astonishment) that people regularly developed strong emotional bonds with the program. In one instance he found that his secretary would insist that he leave the room while she used the program; others were offended when asked to view transcripts of their interactions with the program, claiming it was an invasion of their privacy. According to Weizenbaum, "A number of practicing psychiatrists seriously believed the DOCTOR computer program could grow into a nearly completely automatic form of psychotherapy" (5).

ELIZA's obvious association with the Turing test tends to transform discussion of it into debates over Turing's definition of intelligence. And since ELIZA operates within a realm normally considered part of medical therapy for mental disorders experienced by real human beings, the program adds to this a set of obvious ethical questions. Weizenbaum was undoubtedly correct in stating his objection to the idea that therapists might one day be replaced with machines: "I had thought it essential, as a prerequisite to the very possibility that one person might help another learn to cope with his emotional problems, that the helper himself participate in the other's experience of those problems and, in large part by way of his own empathetic recognition of them, himself come to understand them" (7). The fact that such an argument seemed necessary indicates that at least some users believed ELIZA was capable of helping them. The program has been cited as an example of what Karl Mannheim called the "documentary method" of interpretation, in which appearances are understood to account for an underlying reality that is then used as a source for interpretation of that reality (Suchman 23). But while this might account for the occasions when ELIZA fools people into thinking that their interlocutor is a human, it does not explain instances when the "underlying reality" is understood by everyone involved (including the famous secretary) to be a piece of software wholly incapable of empathetic recognition or understanding. Even if one is fooled by the Turing test, the interaction is permeated with artifice. From the start, the entity on the other side of the wall is "a creature simultaneously animal and machine, who populates worlds ambiguously natural and crafted" (Haraway 150).

In the mid-1960s the American ethnomethodologist Harold Garfinkel conducted an experiment that gives some insight into the specific contours of how one might be fooled by the mingling of text and machine. He asked a group of American college students to agree to be counseled over an intercom. Students could pose questions to the human interlocutor in the form of yes/no responses. What the students did not know is that the pattern of responses was essentially random; that is, an imperative algorithm of the most rudimentary kind—a script that, though read by a human, consisted of a preset pattern of "yes" and "no" for each of the subjects. Here is a partial transcript of one of the interactions in which a male Jewish student asks the "counselor" whether he should continue dating a non-Jewish girl:

> SUBJECT: Okay, this is a situation that I am presented with. I happen to be of the Jewish faith and I have been dating a Gentile girl now for about two months. My dad is not directly opposed to this situation, but I feel at the same time that he is not exactly pleased with it. Mother feels that as long as Dad is not directly opposed to this situation that I should go ahead and continue dating until he makes some direct statement to the contrary. My reason for feeling why he is not too pleased with this is that he will come up with digs and sayings that make me feel very ill at ease about dating the girl. My question is, do you feel under the present circumstances that I should continue or stop dating this girl? Let me put that in a positive way. Do you feel that I should continue dating this girl?
>
> EXPERIMENTER: My answer is no.
>
> SUBJECT: No. Well, that is kind of interesting. I kinda feel that there is really no great animosity between Dad and I but, well, perhaps he feels that greater

dislike will grow out of this. I suppose or maybe it is easier for an outsider to see certain things that I am blind to at this moment.

I would like to ask my second question now.

EXPERIMENTER: Okay.

SUBJECT: Do you feel that I should have a further discussion with Dad about this situation or not? Should I have further discussion with Dad over this subject about dating the Gentile girl?

EXPERIMENTER: My answer is yes.

SUBJECT: Well I feel that is reasonable but I really don't know what to say to him. I mean he seems to be not really too understanding. In other words he seems to be afraid really to discuss the situation. I mean at least it appears that way to me so far. But I guess if it is worthwhile to me, if I really want to continue to date her that I will go on and have this discussion with Dad. I really don't know what to say because I mean I am dating her. I am not in love with her or anything but I really never know what is going to come out. I guess we should have a discussion based on what the future possibilities might be and how he would feel about that. He may not be too strongly opposed now because we are only dating, but perhaps he sees future complications that he would really like to get off his chest at the moment. I am ready for my third question now.

If after having my conversation with Dad and he says to continue dating her, but at the same time he gives me an impression that he is really not, he really does not want me to date her, but he is only doing it because he wants to be a good Dad, should under these conditions, should I still date the girl?

EXPERIMENTER: My answer is yes.

SUBJECT: Well I am actually surprised at the answer. I expected a no answer on that. Perhaps this is because you are not quite aware of my dad and his reactions and he seems to be the type of person that is sensitive and therefore he is very careful in the way that he will handle things. Even though he might have said go ahead and date her I perhaps would feel guilty in knowing that he really did not want me to continue to date her. Though I don't know that it would actually help the situation any. So, well, perhaps we will look into this further and that is another question. (Garfinkel 80–81)

Garfinkel noticed that "Present answers provide answers to further questions that will never be asked," that "Where answers are unsatisfying or incomplete, the subjects are willing to wait for later answers in order to decide the sense of previous ones," and that "When answers are incongruous or contradictory, subjects are able to continue by finding that the 'advisor' has learned more in the meantime, or that he has changed his mind, or that perhaps he is not sufficiently acquainted with the intricacies of the problem, or the fault was in the question so that another phrasing is necessary" (90–91). Even compound questions that are not logically tractable in terms of yes/no answers

were interpreted as appropriate (90). The subject strives at all costs to make
sense of the exchange.

One investigator describes Garfinkel's experimental methodology as
"cold-blooded" (Zeitlyn 192), and, as with ELIZA, the possibility is raised of
something unethical and duplicitous having occurred. Yet it is clear that real
knowledge was gained. One witnesses the subject turning the matter over in
his mind—exploring options, considering alternatives, and generally seeking
a solution to his dilemma. One might argue that a real psychologist capable
of empathy (and permitted to pose questions and answer at length) would be
preferable, but one might also argue that it is precisely the arbitrary nature
of the answers—and their informational paucity—that probes the subject
into considering questions from new angles. Garfinkel's program might even
be thought of, following Marshall McLuhan, as a "cooling off" of the hot
medium of therapy. The inclusive and highly participatory regime of "yes"
and "no" serves to weaken the dominating intensity of interactions, which,
like a loquacious therapist, are more focused on leaving us "well filled with
data" (McLuhan 23). The counselor (or, better, the "program") is incapable of
empathy and therefore impervious to influence flowing in the other direction.
It cannot tell the student what it thinks the student wants to hear. It cannot
avoid uncomfortable or stressful moments in the midst of the exchange.
And because there is very little narrative to the patterns of "yes" and "no,"
the student has to work harder to construct narratives of explanation. Yet it
would be difficult to argue that the student had thought of things "that way"
before entering into the exchange.

Something like this occurs when one considers text-analytical results
generated using imperative routines. If something is known from a word-
frequency list or a data visualization, it is undoubtedly a function of our desire
to make sense of what has been presented. We fill in gaps, make connections
backward and forward, explain inconsistencies, resolve contradictions, and,
above all, generate additional narratives in the form of declarative realizations. Like any reading, readings of imperatively generated results allege
numerous outside contexts and prompt various forms of cathexis. Like all
textual artifacts, they rely upon a prior experience of language and a will
toward sense-making. But like a therapy session with ELIZA, they are suffused with the certain knowledge of something crude lying beneath—a bare
algorithm that cannot allege anything. As with the Turing test, the reader
invariably engages not one text, but two texts operating within an orbit of
fruitful antagonism: the text that creates the results (the code) and the results
themselves. The self-conscious "reader" of ELIZA or the Turing test is not
only responding to the computer's prompts but also evaluating the logic and

appropriateness of those responses. Even if one succumbs to momentary belief, it is not in the same way that one succumbs to the illusions of a horror movie. "It's only a movie" serves to break us out of the dominating force of illusion; "it's only a machine" breaks us in to the doubleness—the divided textual field—that undergirds all computational engagements.

Algorithmic criticism is easily conceived as the form of engagement that results when imperative routines are inserted into the wider constellation of texts stipulated by critical reading. But it is also to be understood as the creation of interactive programs in which readers are forced to contend not only with deformed texts, but with the "how" of those deformations. Algorithmic criticism therefore begins with the machinic inflection of programming—a form of textual creation that, despite the apparent determinism of the underlying machine, proceeds always in organic and unexpected ways. Gilles Deleuze and Félix Guattari might have been describing the creation of such programs in their ethical injunctions toward the Body without Organs (BwO):

> Lodge yourself on a stratum, experiment with the opportunities it offers, find an advantageous place on it, find potential movements of deterritorialization, possible lines of flight, experience them, produce flow conjunctions here and there, try out continuums of intensities segment by segment, have a small plot of new land at all times. It is through meticulous relation with the strata that one succeeds in freeing lines of flight, causing conjugation flows to pass and escape and bringing forth continuous intensities for a BwO. . . . You have constructed your own little machine, ready when needed to be plunged into other collective machines. (161)

The stratum that we lodge ourselves upon with algorithmic criticism is one in which both results and the textual generation of results are systematically manipulated and transformed, connected and reconnected with unlike things. It is by nature a "meticulous" process, since to program is to move within a highly constrained language that is wholly intolerant toward deviation from its own internal rules. But the goal of such constraint is always unexpected forms of knowing within the larger framework of more collective understandings. The algorithmic critic, as the author of the deformation machine from which he or she hopes to draw insight, becomes both the analyst and the analysand—ELIZA's interlocutor and its creator. It is neither immoderate nor facile to suggest that the encroachment of such "little machines" into the space of literary-critical work represents a revolutionary provocation against the methodologies that have guided criticism and philosophy for centuries. The hermeneutics of "what is" becomes mingled with the hermeneutics of "how to."

Students being initiated into the precise discipline in which machines are created and discussed are often asked to write a program that can generate a list of numbers in which each successive number is the sum of the two previous numbers in the sequence:

1   1   2   3   5   8   13   21   34   55   89   144   233 . . .

That this arrangement, which is commonly known as the Fibonacci sequence, would come to be associated with computation—that it would occupy a place only slightly beneath "Hello, world" in the first lispings of computer programmers—is perhaps ironic, given that the sequence first came to light in Europe in a book largely concerned with teaching others how to perform calculations effectively by hand. The name comes from the nickname of the author, Leonardo Pisano (c. 1170-c. 1250), whose *Liber Abaci* contains not only the famous sequence (embedded in a fanciful problem involving the breeding of rabbits) but also the first successful popularization of the *modus Indorum:* the nine "Indian figures" that form the elementary units of the base-ten number system.[3] It is an ancient observation. The great Hindu grammarian Pingala, who called it *mātrāmeru,* or "the mountain of cadence," observed it in the metrical rhythms of Sanskrit more than two thousand years ago, and it has been rediscovered many times since. Over the centuries, the ratios implicit in the sequence (which, in a strange bit of mathematical serendipity, converge toward the "golden ratio" of 1.6180339887) have been observed in everything from the pattern of spirals on a pine cone to the long-term behavior of the stock market.

Before computers, most people would have understood the "how to" of the sequence as a text that descends in part from Fibonacci's vital moment of cultural appropriation. Today it is a trivial matter to represent the generalized form of the Fibonacci sequence using standard mathematical notation:

$$F(n) := \begin{cases} 0 & \text{if } n = 0 \\ 1 & \text{if } n = 1 \\ F(n-1) + F(n-2) & \text{if } n > 1 \end{cases}$$

But this apparently simple equation contains a deeply subtle and difficult-to-understand relationship that becomes evident only when one notices that F is part of the definition of F. In order to "solve" F for any value of n greater than 1, we need to apply the equation to itself. But how can one begin the process of understanding an equation that requires an understanding of the equation? We could work it out on paper by substituting various numbers for *n* and trying to figure out how the equation works. That would perhaps convince us that the equation is correct, but our scribblings would not have the character of generalization evident in the formula. What is needed, then, is not a mathematical text, but an algorithmic text:

```
(define (fib n)
    (cond ((= n 0) 0)
        ((= n 1) 1)
        (else (+ (fib (– n 1))
            (fib (– n 2))))))
```

In one sense the difference is merely notational; even someone who is not familiar with the syntax of Scheme (the dialect of Lisp in which this program is written) can discern some of the same relationships that are expressed in the standard equation. As with the equation, the function *(fib n)* is defined in terms of *(fib n)*. But this notation possesses an explanatory power that is difficult to achieve with mathematical notation. The former tells us that the definition of *F* for numbers greater than 1 is related to *F* in a particular way; the latter describes a process in which we move step-by-step through the relationship itself. At a certain point, while reading the program, we find ourselves needing to go back to where we started in order to continue. At another point, we can no longer continue. And as we move through the notation, we generate the sequence in question.

One might be tempted to say that what becomes known in the process of computing the Fibonacci sequence is simply a method by which one may generate the sequence. "Learning to program" is undoubtedly the process of learning such methods, and recursion is simply one way of accomplishing the stated goal. But while both the equation and the program lead one ultimately toward appreciation of a pattern implicit in the natural numbers (the formal definition of which is also recursive), the two notations differ profoundly in terms of the type of knowing that each one both illuminates and demands. Harold Abelson and Gerald Sussman, in *The Structure and Interpretation of Computer Programs,* explain: "The contrast between function and procedure is a reflection of the general distinction between describing properties of things and describing how to do things, or, as it is sometimes referred to, the distinction between declarative knowledge and imperative knowledge. In mathematics, we are usually concerned with declarative (what is) descriptions, whereas in computer science we are usually concerned with imperative (how to) descriptions" (26). Mathematics undergirds computing at every turn, and yet "executable mathematics" is more dream than reality for designers of programming languages. Even Scheme, which is frequently thought of as a "functional" language (as opposed to a mostly imperative language like C), cannot but make plain the difference between a text that describes a relationship and one that can perform the relationships it describes. Yet the difference remains an epistemological one. If code represents a radical form of textuality, it is not merely because of what it allows us to do but also because of the way it allows us to think.

Writing software that deforms texts in order to facilitate interpretation therefore places the critic in the midst of a peculiar form of textual apprehension. In order to write the program, the critic must consider the "how to" of a deformative operation, but once that text is written, the output will be one that places the same critic into a critical relationship not only with the text of the result but with the text of the program as well. It is one thing to suspect (as with ELIZA) that something not quite human lies beneath the text from which one is drawing insight; it is another thing entirely to be the creator of that same monster. On the one hand, the process is iterative. The results modify our conceptions, which in turn help to modify the program that generated them. But in another sense it is a recursive process. In order to understand the text we must create another text that requires an understanding of the first text. The former might suggest analogies with science, but the latter suggests analogy with the deepest philosophical questions of the humanities, including the hermeneutic circle that has so preoccupied poststructuralist thought.

That these recursions might represent useful critical engagements, apart from any definitive result they might yield, was driven home to me a few years ago. I was attempting to write a program that could draw directed graphs of the scene changes in Shakespeare's plays. The program needed to divide the text of the plays into their constituent scenes so the program could render a visualization in which each scene was a node in a network (with lines between the nodes indicating the passage from one location in a play to another). It was not long before I began to realize that even the simplest aspects of this operation were fraught with ambiguity:

> Things are easy, when, as in *Twelfth Night,* Shakespeare proceeds from the Duke's palace (Act I, Scene i) to the Seacoast (Act I, Scene ii). It's a lot more difficult to say what a scene is when Shakespeare says (as he does in *The Tempest*) that it takes place in "another part of island" or (as in *As You Like It*) "a room in the palace." Is it the same part of the island we were looking at the last time we were at the other part of the island, or a new part? Can we assume that the Duke is speaking to his Lords in the same place where Celia and Rosalind have lately had their *tête-à-tête,* or would it make more sense to have it occur in a different place? What, after all, is a "place" in a play? A nineteenth-century

performance on the proscenium stage at Covent Garden might have let us know by a physical change of scenery (or perhaps not, in a production of *Love's Labour's Lost* where the entire play takes place in various parts of "The King of Navarre's Park"). What we know of Shakespeare's own stage would lead us to believe that such matters were left mainly to the audience, there being nothing but changes in character and costume to suggest a change of scene. And, of course, editors of Shakespeare's plays do not uniformly agree on the scene divisions. *Antony and Cleopatra,* a play notable for its rapid scene changes and wide-ranging settings, had no typographical indications of scene divisions at all until 1709. (Ramsay 181–82)

Such conundrums are not unique either to Shakespeare's plays or to criticism itself. The confusing nature of Shakespeare's scene divisions are (and have been) an obvious occasion for reflection, since such apparently straightforward matters as "where does the scene start?" have a palpable effect on the way we read and understand them. A careful editor has the ability to facilitate that discussion by noting the "instability" of the text itself in a critical apparatus. Both activities allow for—and, indeed, thrive upon—ambiguity.

The computer, though, demands an answer. And while many have argued that the computer's demand is a reasonable one—a chance for literary critics to "get the facts straight"—such a vision of the computer tends to mistake the nature of critical inquiry. Neither the critic nor the editor (to say nothing of the theorist or the teacher) seeks a definitive answer to the questions posed by the apparently simple matter of where scenes begin and end, because criticism is concerned not with determining the facts of the text, but with the implications of the text in its potentialized form. The computer, if it is to participate at all, can only serve to broaden that potentiality. Even if the computer proposes facts, they will be relegated by the episteme of humanistic inquiry to the status of further evidence (which is to say, further opportunity for reflection). Questions will be raised about any possible choice. Suspicions will arise about the machinic text that underlies the apparent. Yet even as we consider such matters, the computer waits. It still demands an answer.

The computer's role is only to ask how our engagements might be facilitated, but it does so with a staggering range of provisos and conditions. Upon opening a programming manual, one discovers that all data must be expressed as strings or numbers; that ontologies may only take the form of lists, trees, or matrices; that everything is an object of a certain class. And over and above these, the computer demands abstraction and encapsulation of its components. The computer wants to know whether *Jane Eyre* is an object of type Novel with composed objects of type Chapter, Paragraph, Sentence, and Word, or whether *Jane Eyre* is a data stream that can act as the parameter to a function. Even if we are loath to regard texts as being, in the words of one commentator, "ordered hierarchies of content objects" (DeRose), we must acknowledge that this is the way the computer would prefer to have it. Dino Buzetti, in pondering the nature of computational representations like XML, rightly concludes that "the computational notion of a text as a type of data does not coincide with the notion of the text as a product of literary activity" (61), and though he confidently calls for a digital content model that would achieve such a correspondence, it is not at all clear, assuming the present theory of computation, that such a model exists. We murder to compute.

We sometimes imagine that if computers are to participate in human discourse, they must evince the freedom of that discourse. Yet that discourse—much like the dialogues generated by Turing and Weizenbaum—is suffused with constraint and stricture. Upon preparing to compose a sonnet, one discovers that it must be written in iambic pentameter and must adhere to a rigid rhyme scheme. On preparing to write a novel, one notices that convention—historically a mighty, almost irrepressible constraint—imposes the existence of characters, dialogue, and plot. If one is to write, one is perforce constrained to words. One might argue that literary history is as much about rebellion from such strictures as compliance, but one could also say that the history of programming is likewise the history of rebellions that occur not in spite of the constraints but because of them. The word processor or Web browser does not inhere in the material. It is not, as Michelangelo is said to have believed, a matter of chipping away all that is not the sculpture. To contend with the "how to" of programming is to discover the potentialities of constraint. To read the outputted text is to do the same.

Few texts illustrate this principle better than the Turing test itself, which proposes a set of rigid boundaries upon the otherwise open-ended question, "Can machines think?" That we have been debating that question in terms of the parameters set forth by the test for half a century is testament enough to its power to provoke discussion and debate. But for Turing, the conceptual spirit behind the wall was the Turing machine—the result of another thought experiment, which, if less well known, has nonetheless had a still greater impact on the development of the idea of computation. That machine, after all, had falsified the *Entscheidungsproblem* and declared insuperable limits to mathematics itself. It is difficult to imagine that Turing's test for intelligence was not itself borne of the earth-shattering limitations of this primal, primitive machine. Given that this failure is largely responsible for the revolution that ensued, algorithmic criticism might well eschew the question of success and instead ask how much more gloriously and fruitfully it might fail. The goal, after all, is not to arrive at the truth, as science strives to do. In literary criticism, as in the humanities more generally, the goal has always been to arrive at the question.

5 'PATACOMPUTING

A few years ago, Martin Mueller, the animating force behind the text analysis system *WordHoard*, decided to perform what we might call an experiment but would better be thought of as the fulfillment of a brief moment of curiosity. Using the system's powerful word-counting and lemmatization features, Mueller was able to create lists of the most frequent words in Homer and Shakespeare:

Homer	Shakespeare
man (ἀνήρ)	lord
ship (ναῦς)	man
god (θέος)	sir
heart (θῦμός)	love
hand (χείρ)	king
son (υἱός)	heart
horse (ἵππος)	eye
father (πᾰτήρ)	time
word (ἔπος)	hand
companion (ἑταῖρος)	father

I call attention to the spur-of-the-moment character of his investigations, not to suggest that one could not conduct elaborate experiments involving word frequency (many have done so), but simply to point out the ways in which this operation has been made virtually effortless by digital technology. The creation of *WordHoard* required many hours of careful programming and design, but that effort is minimal in comparison to what was required of those who created the first dictionaries and concordances—or even, for that matter, the first books. If Alfred North Whitehead was correct, the result of such effortlessness represents not just the formation of a new convenience but also an epochal moment for civilization, which, he thought, "advances by adding to the number of important operations which we can perform without thinking about them" (42).

It is appropriate, of course, that we ask whether Mueller's lists are the result of an "important operation." They do not contain anything that one might call, at first glance, an astonishing result, and one immediately intuits facile lines of argument proceeding from them. Homer's *Iliad*, after all, is a book "about ships" only in the way that the old bromide figures *Moby Dick* to be a book "about fishing." It comes as a surprise to no one that God and man are subjects of concern to both Homer and Shakespeare. The lists seem "right," but the knowledge we gain by their revelation might be thought of as confirming what we already know. For Mueller, it is both more and less than what we expect: "Given the fact that writers spend endless hours putting their words into the right order, it is disconcerting that a list of their most commonly used nouns will tell you quite a bit about what they are up to. This grossly reductive model of a text works much better than it should. . . . Homer is about 'man, ship, and god' in that order. Stop reading right there" ("Digital Shakespeare" 12). That we can arrive at a three-word précis of the *Iliad* "without thinking" seems of little moment if the result of such critical operations leads to "grossly reductive models." In every way, the un-deformed text seems preferable to its atomized form.

Still, it is unlikely that a human being, even if asked to name only the top three words in each text, would produce these lists precisely as the machine gives them to us. And for this reason, our explanations must assume the character of narrative. Perhaps "eye" figures prominently in Shakespeare because, as Maurice Charney observed, "Love enters through the eye" (122), with the result that romantic protagonists in Shakespeare are no longer masters of themselves but instead subject to forces not of their own making—forces different from, but related to, the forces that perturb the lives of Achilles, Hector, and Odysseus. One might also observe that the "heart" of Homer is not at all the "heart" of Shakespeare. *Thumos* is soul, vitality, spiritedness—the *animus* of the body. It is also the will to distinguish oneself—the horse that runs alongside *eros* in the Plato's *Phaedrus* and that will appear centuries later in Evagrius's description of the "passions." At some point we must contend with the anomalies. Why is "hand" so prominent in both lists? "Love" and "time" seem right for a Renaissance dramatist, but the explanation of both words will require much more elaborate explanations. Mueller notes that "'love' and 'time' mark out important semantic domains of Shakespeare and indeed of 'modern' literature as it has been theorized since the Quarrel of the Ancients and Moderns" ("Digital Shakespeare" 13). But what are these semantic domains?

Other algorithmic processes suggest themselves. *WordHoard* can unerringly (and instantaneously) locate every instance of "love" and "time" in both texts—even distinguishing the noun from the verb in the case of the former. Given such marvels, it is tempting to suppose that one might even settle the Quarrel, as it were, by using tools that were unavailable to any scholar before now. But in fact, further transformative operations are most likely to follow the same course that Mueller's lists set for us. The results (the new lists) would first hit us with the force of the obvious while at the same time causing us to construct narratives that, despite the "obviousness" of the results, must at a certain point adjust to the parts that don't quite fit or that require more elaborate explanations. An analogy with science suggests itself, but not the usual analogy. Throughout the process, and largely in spite of ourselves, we would teeter between confirming our own theories and forming new ones. At a certain point our narrative could no longer be said to resemble the one that supposedly explained the very thing that threatened to make us "stop reading right there."

Algorithmic criticism is born at that moment, but it need not be born. David Hoover—a skilled stylometrist, and therefore a great lover of lists—likes to play a game with his students in which he shows them a list of novels and asks them to rank them according to "vocabulary richness" (defined as the largest number of different words per fifty-thousand-word block):[1]

Faulkner	*Light in August*
Henry James	*The Ambassadors*
Bram Stoker	*Dracula*
D. H. Lawrence	*Sons and Lovers*
Oscar Wilde	*The Picture of Dorian Gray*
Virginia Woolf	*To the Lighthouse*
Willa Cather	*My Ántonia*
H. G. Wells	*The War of the Worlds*
Jack London	*The Sea Wolf*
Mark Twain	*Pudd'nhead Wilson*
Rudyard Kipling	*Kim*
Sinclair Lewis	*Main Street*

A few years ago, in an e-mail in which he offered this list for the edification of my own students, Hoover suggested that I "see how they react to the fact that they are listed in ASCENDING order of vocabulary richness." "What always really astonishes them," he wrote, "is that Sinclair Lewis has double the vocabulary of Faulkner" ("Face of Text"). My students are indeed astonished by this. Faulkner, as every undergraduate student knows, is hard; *Main Street* is straightforward. James is notoriously "wordy" (more so even than Wilde);

The Sea Wolf is simple and fun; *Kim* is a children's book. The professional scholars to whom I have shown this list, however, are eager to point out how un-astonished they are. Mostly they complain about "richness"—sometimes accusing me of having rigged the game (though I am careful to explain the precise definition of "richness" being stipulated). Not one of them has ever gotten the order remotely correct.

As with Mueller's lists, one is behooved to go further by examining the language from which these results are drawn. Here is the prologue to *Main Street,* which, Hoover assured me, "helps explain it":

> The town is, in our tale, called "Gopher Prairie, Minnesota." But its Main Street is the continuation of Main Streets everywhere. The story would be the same in Ohio or Montana, in Kansas or Kentucky or Illinois, and not very differently would it be told Up York State or in the Carolina hills.
>
> Main Street is the climax of civilization. That this Ford car might stand in front of the Bon Ton Store, Hannibal invaded Rome and Erasmus wrote in Oxford cloisters. What Ole Jenson the grocer says to Ezra Stowbody the banker is the new law for London, Prague, and the unprofitable isles of the sea; whatsoever Ezra does not know and sanction, that thing is heresy, worthless for knowing and wicked to consider.
>
> Our railway station is the final aspiration of architecture. Sam Clark's annual hardware turnover is the envy of the four counties which constitute God's Country. In the sensitive art of the Rosebud Movie Palace there is a Message, and humor strictly moral.
>
> Such is our comfortable tradition and sure faith. Would he not betray himself an alien cynic who should otherwise portray Main Street, or distress the citizens by speculating whether there may not be other faiths? (Lewis 4)

And here are the second and third paragraphs of Faulkner's *Light in August:*

> She had never even been to Doane's Mill until after her father and mother died, though six or eight times a year she went to town on Saturday, in the wagon, in a mail-order dress and her bare feet flat in the wagon bed and her shoes wrapped in a piece of paper beside her on the seat. She would put on the shoes just before the wagon reached town. After she got to be a big girl she would ask her father to stop the wagon at the edge of town and she would get down and walk. She would not tell her father why she wanted to walk in instead of riding. He thought that it was because of the smooth streets, the sidewalks. But it was because she believed that the people who saw her and whom she passed on foot would believe that she lived in the town too.
>
> When she was twelve years old her father and mother died in the same summer, in a log house of three rooms and a hall, without screens, in a room lighted by a bug-swirled kerosene lamp, the naked floor worn smooth as old

silver by naked feet. She was the youngest living child. Her mother died first. Then he died. McKinley, the brother, arrived in a wagon. They buried the father in a grove behind a country church one afternoon, with a pine headstone. The next morning she departed forever, though it is possible that she did not know this at the time, in the wagon with McKinley, for Doane's Mill. The wagon was borrowed and the brother had promised to return it by nightfall. (3–4)

There is no sense in which these excerpts "explain" the lists; at best, they demonstrate more clearly what the lists tell us. That is undoubtedly all that Hoover meant to convey. What needs explaining is not the fact that the vocabularies differ, or even that our perceptions differ from some supposed textual reality. The explanations we need run instead along two opposite poles separating the astonishment of the students from the skepticism of the scholars.

My students have no trouble explaining why the lists surprise them, but their reactions—unencumbered by the professional consequences of error—give us the seeds of a kind of exploration seldom associated with text analysis. They have arrayed the objects of their intellectual life in categories that correspond, among other things, to the cultural penumbras in which texts are disseminated and taught. Books come to them as high or low, deep or shallow, hard or easy, read "for pleasure" or read "for class," with dozens of gradations in between, and they assume (rightly) that words are somehow, though not exclusively, implicated in this arrangement. The scholars, by contrast, are eager to construct a narrative by which the new results can fit with what they already know—an activity they undertake confidently and with ease. For the students, the game has not risen to the level of criticism. For the scholars, it has not descended far enough toward circumspection. The scholars are right to interrogate the admittedly crude notion of "richness" stipulated by the game, but to stop there is to avoid algorithmic criticism. What is needed is a definition of "richness" that can account not merely for the professional reaction but also for the reactions of the students. The result of such investigations might be a better game (or a better algorithm), but it is just as likely to involve critical investigations that, like the confusing confluence of words and culture, do not involve computational analysis. The ultimate result, in other words, is the conversation itself, which is neither content with the "imagine that" of disrupted expectations nor too eager to explain it all away.

Bolder methods are required if we are to break away from these two impulses, and in recent years a number of new tools have appeared that aim to negotiate such territory. One of the more elaborate ones is the *Text Analysis Portal for Research (TAPoR),* which cheerfully employs metaphors that are entirely foreign to contemporary humanistic inquiry. Methods for analyzing "the theoretical basis of texts," "exploring themes," and "comparing concepts" are presented as "recipes" with numbered steps (Rockwell, "TAPoR Recipes"). We're invited to "try it" as if the thing to try were a new car or a new pill. Again and again, the language of *TAPoR* points not to methods or procedures, but to "tools"—things to be wielded against any text on the Web (the default examples optimistically include both a corpus of French medieval poetry and the *Universal Declaration of Human Rights*). Yet despite these metaphors, all of which mingle marketing with mechanization in a way that suggests anything other than the sober, meandering *parole* of humanistic discourse, *TAPoR* confidently asserts a rhetoric of self-interrogation. In one of *TAPoR's* apologias, we read that text analysis involves "asking questions of a text and retrieving passages that help one *think through the questions*" (Rockwell "What Is Text Analysis?"; emphasis mine). Concordances, keyword-in-context displays, frequency generators, and even a "word cloud" that sets the tokens adrift in a two-dimensional space are presented as provocations designed to force users into "think[ing] about their interpretative practices." However foreign its interface might be, text analysis is insistently put forth by *TAPoR* as "an interactive practice of discovery with its own serendipitous paths comparable to, but not identical to, the serendipitous discovery that happens in rereading a text." (Rockwell, "What Is Text Analysis?")

Few tools better illustrate these serendipitous paths than Stéfan Sinclair's *HyperPo,* one of the tools for which *TAPoR* acts as a portal. From the first moment a text is loaded into *HyperPo,* it is transformed into data points and visualizations. The very first screen is a kind of neoteric frontispiece in which the text—in this case, Christina Rossetti's *Goblin Market*—is presented as a series of critical statistics:

Report on the Text

- Text Source: goblin.txt
- Text Title: Goblin Market
- Language of text: English
- Total words (tokens): 3107
- Unique words (types): 1130
- Highest word frequency: 124
- Average word frequency: 2.75
- Standard Deviation of word frequencies: 7.58
- Average word length: 4.30
- Standard Deviation of word lengths: 1.82
- Number of sentences: 77
- Average words per sentence: 40.4
- Number of paragraphs: 568
- Average words per paragraph: 5.5

Such numbers are seldom meaningful without context, but they invite us into contexts that are possible only with digital tools. One would like to ask whether Rossetti's average word length is long or short relative to other poems written by her, other poems of the period, or to other poems in the English language, even though it is not at all clear where such investigations would lead or what the results might mean. Even so, seeing some trend or sudden spike in the graph along any of these vectors would prompt further questions that extend beyond the linguistic or even the stylistic. *Goblin Market,* after all, is not merely an example of nineteenth-century word usage. It is, within the widening context of critical thought, a children's poem, an erotic poem, a Victorian poem, a feminist poem, a pre-Raphaelite poem, and a poem about market forces at mid-century. We cannot avoid reading such considerations "into the data." If algorithmic criticism is to occur, we must insist upon it.

If crossing the broad terms of textual discussion with frequencies and deviations has not yet invited critics to such speculation, it is perhaps because such lists as these evoke critical procedures that are long out of fashion. This is perhaps why *HyperPo,* true to its name, presents them only briefly as a kind of parlor trick. It is the last moment in which confident assertions of fact prevail. At the bottom of the list we are invited to "Continue" on to an interface in which there is no way to encounter the text on its own. In the upper left is a box in which the words of the texts—now better thought of as "tokens"—have been colorized by frequency. In the upper right is a box for word frequency lists, which are always connected back to the deformed text through hyperlinks. The lower box displays graphs and charts, and they, too, are linked to the other windows. Clicking on any word in any part of the interface tends to set off chain reactions in others. So while we might try to read *Goblin Market,* that reading will soon be interrupted by a "weighted centroid"—a visualization in which each word is pulled off from a center point, as if by a gravitational force, by the words that surround it. Dozens of interruptions are offered. The strangest (whimsically labeled as an "advanced option") is undoubtedly the one that lets the user generate all anagrams contained within the text:

- ache (2), each (6)
- any (3), nay (3)
- are (2), ear (2)
- ate (3), eat (5)
- bore (1), robe (1)
- dare (1), dear (2)
- felt (2), left (1)
- for (22), fro (1)
- golden (11), longed (2)

- how (5), who (3)
- its (5), sit (1)
- lemons (1), melons (3)
- listen (1), silent (1)
- made (1), mead (1)
- mane (1), name (1)
- nails (1), snail (3)
- night (11), thing (1)
- owls (1), slow (1)
- rose (1), sore (3)
- saw (1), was (11)
- stone (5), tones (2)

As with Saussure's anagrams, we are likely to view such results with a mixture of suspicion and fascination. Taken alone, they seem either to represent evidence of a peculiar but undeniable property of English orthography (and therefore are essentially meaningless as a set of collocates), or as the gateway to a dubious mysticism. In the context of *HyperPo*, however, such results serve to deepen a relationship with the text that governs the entire experience of using the tool. For all its concern with numerical information, *HyperPo* consciously works against the realization of "results." Instead, we engage in a kind of "microscopic reading," which, like the close reading it both analogizes and contradicts, draws us into certain kinds of noticings. Clicking through various collocates and word properties, for example, one notices that "Laura" collocates with "should" and "Lizzie" collocates with "not"; that the word "evil" appears in the poem, but not the word "good"; that "suck" is strongly collocated not only with "me," but also with "them"; that there is a steady upward increase (punctuated with various gaps) in instances of the word "eyes."

We might think of these as the "facts" of the text, but whatever knowledge is gained from their perusal stands at a marked distance from the quest for factuality that usually motivates linguistic and philological inquiry. Lizzie's sexually charged experiences and the refrain of the goblin men ("Come buy, come buy") might lead one to focus on these features, but even as one tries to follow these threads, the frames blink in and out with patterns and associations that lead in other (often contradictory) directions. *Explication de texte* is surely one possible outcome from these procedures, but the *texte* of *HyperPo* does not allow one to rest upon any straightforward set of heuristic prompts or frameworks. There are too many gaps—too many incentives for narrative—to allow one to ignore the extratextual valences that had once been rejected by the New Criticism. *Goblin Market* becomes what Jacques

Derrida, in "*Ulysses* Gramophone," called an "overpotentialized text": "We are caught in the net. All the gestures sketched in to allow an initiatory movement are already announced in an overpotentialized text that will remind you, at a given moment, that you are captive in a language, writing, knowledge, and even narration network" (48). In the end, it is this text that constitutes the "result" produced by *HyperPo*: the text reframed by the "serendipitous discovery" of rereading.

Text analysis of the sort put forth by *WordHoard, TAPoR,* and *HyperPo* suggests other antonyms to close reading, including what Franco Moretti has called "distant reading." For Moretti, such reading is not merely a new possibility suggested by the sudden abundance of digitized texts, but, rather, a necessity for any coherent study of world literature:

> [T]he trouble with close reading (in all of its incarnations, from the new criticism to deconstruction) is that it necessarily depends on an extremely small canon. This may have become an unconscious and invisible premiss [*sic*] by now, but it is an iron one nonetheless: you invest so much in individual texts *only* if you think that very few of them really matter. Otherwise, it doesn't make sense. And if you want to look beyond the canon (and of course, world literature will do so: it would be absurd if it didn't!) close reading will not do it. It's not designed to do it, it's designed to do the opposite. At bottom, it's a theological exercise—very solemn treatment of very few texts taken very seriously—whereas what we really need is a little pact with the devil: we know how to read texts, now let's learn how *not* to read them. Distant reading: where distance, let me repeat it, *is a condition of knowledge:* it allows you to focus on units that are much smaller or much larger than the text: devices, themes, tropes—or genres and systems. And if, between the very small and the very large, the text itself disappears, well, it is one of those cases when one can justifiably say, Less is more. If we want to understand the system in its entirety, we must accept losing something. We always pay a price for theoretical knowledge: reality is infinitely rich; concepts are abstract, are poor. But it's precisely this 'poverty' that makes it possible to handle them, and therefore to know. This is why less is actually more. ("Conjectures" 57)

That we might "lose the text" undoubtedly frightens many. But as Moretti makes clear, this fear is simply the inverse of the one in which we place our faith. To say that the gypsy interlude in book 12 of *Tom Jones* metaphorically encapsulates a vast network of political tensions in eighteenth-century England strikes us as a responsible use of literature; a spreadsheet full of numerical information on the appearance of "gypsies" in English novels provokes fear of a criticism ungrounded in the particularities of language and textuality. Neither one avoids the hermeneutical circle that has worried every critical theorist since Schleiermacher, but the latter touches not only on fears of an inhumanistic technology but also on our (historically recent) sense of reading as a pious, wholesome activity that can serve to better us.

Most horrifying of all, of course, is the "not reading" that serves as the center of Pierre Bayard's *How to Talk about Books You Haven't Read*. For Martin Mueller, though, this most indecent of all literary anti-procedures becomes an important part of "the query potential of the digital surrogate":

> A book sits in a network of transactions that involve a reader, his interlocutors, and a "collective library" of things one knows or is supposed to know. Felicitous reading—I adapt the term from John Austin's definition of felicitous speech acts—is the art of locating with sufficient precision the place a given book occupies in that network at a given moment. Your skill as a reader, then, is measured by the speed and accuracy with which you can do that. Ideally you should do it in "no time at all." Once you have oriented a book in the right place of its network, you can stop reading. In fact, you should stop reading. . . ."Close reading" has . . . always been an exceptional activity. ("Digital Shakespeare " 9–10)

Many have observed that the affordances offered by digital text archives represent a radical break with conventional reading practices. For Mueller, however, those affordances may represent an enhancement of older forms of "not reading," since large digital corpora "do exactly what older forms of 'not-reading' were supposed to do: orient a text or set of texts in a larger document space" ("Digital Shakespeare" 10). Performing text analysis on a larger document space achieves both objectives simultaneously, since whatever orientation we achieve is largely the result of disorientation.

It is manifestly impossible to read everything, and it has always been so. The utility of the digital corpus—despite its vaunted claims of "increased access"—only serves to make the impossibility of comprehensive reading more apparent (though a stroll through the stacks of even a modest library serves to illustrate the same point). What is different about digital archives is the way in which text analytical procedures (including that most primitive of procedures: the keyword search) has the potential to draw unexpected paths through a documentary space that is distinguished by its overall incomprehensibility. Even Vannevar Bush, amid a conception of hypertext still more sophisticated than that offered by the World Wide Web, imagines the negotiation of the document space as it has been for centuries. Paths are drawn through books that have already been read by others using a relatively weak framework of citation and hearsay. Text analysis, because it allows navigation of the unread and the unknown, focuses the energies of not reading upon structures that lie outside and beneath the spare, if still massive, structures of knowledge represented by the index, the bibliography, and the annotation. Mueller's "top ten words," Hoover's "vocabulary richness," and Sinclair's "weighted centroids" are able to disrupt not because they lay claim to deep textual truths, but because they are capable of presenting the bare, trivial truths of textuality in a way that allows connection with other narratives—in particular, those narratives that seek to install the text into a network of critical activity.

One of the most challenging—and necessary—modulations occurs when the "bare facts" of textuality are self-consciously connected to the insistently subjective aspects of rereading. One experiment, conducted a few years ago as part of the MONK (Metadata Offer New Knowledge) Project used a number of text-mining algorithms to try to discern patterns of "sentimentality" in a group of American novels. The MONK interface presented users with five texts: *Uncle Tom's Cabin, Incidents in the Life of a Slave Girl, Charlotte: A Tale of Truth, Charlotte's Daughter,* and *The Minister's Wooing.* A number of literary critics were then asked to rate passages on a scale in terms of the degree to which they exemplified "sentimentality." The system then analyzed the low-level features of those texts to construct a model that could predict unknown instances. It would not be inaccurate to refer to such a system as a "sentimentality detector," and in general such algorithms (to quote Mueller again) work better than they should. It is the same technology that can locate, with eerie prescience, the books or movies that one "might also like" on websites like Amazon.com and Netflix. But whenever I have had the opportunity to present such systems to my colleagues, I have been confronted with the same question: who decides what sentimentality is?

That question goes a long way toward explaining the social and cultural obstacles to algorithmic criticism. On the one hand, it would seem to imply that "sentimentality" is something that needs to be succinctly defined before attempting to identify it in a particular passage—we define "sentimentality" and then we go find it in texts. Yet at the same time, the question would seem to indicate anxiety over the possibility of succinct definition. Do the people using MONK—the "domain experts," as a computer scientist or usability expert might call them—come to the system with a definition already in place, or is that definition itself the result of reading the texts and "rating" the passages? Won't the definition of "sentimentality" be colored by the dispositions of individual scholars? And who gets to be one of the scholars magisterially defining "sentimentality" for the detector? Isn't the entire idea of a "sentimentality detector" flawed from the start, since "meaning" is itself a shifting, culturally located concept incapable of precise definition or stable articulation? Such questions represent a "stop right there" of a different sort. For in this moment of disbelief and worry, the philosophical insights and anxieties of poststructuralism threaten to do what they rarely do in the normative context of a critical article or scholarly debate. In those contexts, concerns about definition, bias, power, and exception do not halt debate, but guide it more fruitfully. Here, they threaten to dismiss a critical procedure that is distinguished only by the presence of a computer. For surely there is nothing in the procedure that makes any claim to truth value beyond what is already stipulated by any critical act.

The "result" of a system like *MONK* is the same as that for virtually any text-analytical procedure: a textual artifact that, even if recapitulated in the form of an elaborate interactive visualization, remains essentially a list. The algorithm determined that "die," "sorrow," "beloved," and "agony" were indicative of sentimentality. It also isolated "tomorrow," "paternal," and "payment." The first list assures us that there's some validity to the model; like "man, ship, god," it tells us what we already know. The second list, though, is the crucial one. We might say that it reveals what we didn't know; however, that is only a momentary condition. As with any text-analytical result, we can weave a narrative through the gaps. For this reason, we would do better to say that it carves a new path through the document space, which in turn allows us to reread and rethink sentimentality. New definitions are one possible outcome of that rethinking, but the iterative nature of text-analytical tools and the disruptive nature of hyperpoetic texts mirror the iterations and disruptions of critical debate itself. There is no end to our understanding of sentimentality. There are only new noticings, which in this case are practically discernible only through algorithmic means.

It may be that the tools of algorithmic criticism are like Wittgenstein's ladder. When we have used them to "climb up beyond," we recognize them as nonsensical and cast the ladder aside (*Tractatus* 74). The hyperpoetic text, after all, is less concerned with results than with experiences, and for a discipline not especially focused on methodology, it seems tedious—perhaps even pedantic—to detail the terms of that experience as if one were dutifully reporting the parameters of an experimental protocol. Geoffrey Rockwell and Stéfan Sinclair, in an essay titled "There's a Toy in My Essay! Problems with the Rhetoric of Text Analysis," suggest that text analysis "may have to abandon the essay and monograph for an interactive hybrid that can sustain two threads, showing both conclusions and the processes used to reach them." It is not difficult to imagine such a machine; no technical revolution is necessary before we can embed tools like *HyperPo* into a narrative. But neither would it require a rhetorical revolution. The interactive nature of the embedded artifact would allow the reader to arrive at conclusions that are contrary to those being put forth by the narrative that surrounds it. The instant availability of the hyperpoetic text would sew the seeds of the essay's own destruction. The text would become a hybridized offshoot of the larger document space within which it is already implicated. And in that moment, algorithmic criticism would reveal itself most clearly as literary criticism.

If algorithmic criticism does not exist, or exists only in nascent form, it is not because our critical practices are computationally intractable, but because our computational practices have not yet been made critically tractable. To the degree that *WordHoard, TAPoR, HyperPo,* and *MONK* show the way forward, they do so largely by embracing the contingencies that once threatened the discipline of rhetoric, but that, like rhetoric, may come to form the basis for new kinds of critical acts. In an age when the computer itself has gone from being a cold arbiter of numerical facts to being a platform for social networking and self-expression, we may well wonder whether those new kinds of critical acts are in fact already implicit in the many interfaces that seek only to facilitate thought, self expression, and community. As with such recent inventions, the transforming effect will come through "the change of scale, or pace, or pattern that it introduces into human affairs" (McLuhan 8). Once those changes are acknowledged, the bare facts of the tools themselves will seem, like the technical details of automobiles or telephones, not to be the main thing at all. In this sense, algorithmic criticism looks forward not to the widespread acknowledgment of its utility but to the day when "algorithmic criticism" seems as odd a term as "library-based criticism." For by then we will have understood computer-based criticism to be what it has always been: human-based criticism with computers.

POSTCONDITIONS

In many respects, digital humanities is a scholarly discipline like any other. It has, first and foremost, a community with a history. It also has books and journals, scholarly societies, yearly conferences, sources of funding, programs, curricula, students, faculty, and a vast network of scholars both traditional and nontraditional. In this respect, it is more or less like history, or English, or philosophy, or mathematics. In the early 1990s, when debates raged over whether digital humanities (or humanities computing, as it was then called) was, in fact, its own discipline, those who wished to reply affirmatively pointed to these institutional signs as evidence. We are a discipline, they argued, because we are just like all the others.

Some, though, felt certain that we were not at all like the others. To start with, we were radically interdisciplinary. Our conferences, journals, programs, and networks consisted not only of people with backgrounds in all of the traditional humanities disciplines but from engineering, mathematics, and the sciences as well. What's more, the community contained a great number of people who were not traditional research faculty at all (librarians and technical support staff, for example), many of whom were important leaders and innovators in the field. Humanities computing might be a meta-field, or a methodological commons, or a temporary vector for interdisciplinary collaboration, but it surely was not what most of us, in one way or another, had left behind.

That we might have left something behind—with all the fear and uncertainty but also with the joy and liberation that entails—was undoubtedly one of the unacknowledged reasons for this discussion. Some people, who felt betrayed in one way or another by the disciplines in which they had been trained, were eager to plant a flag on the new shore. Others saw this as a way to revivify the tired discourses to which they still felt deeply attached. No one thought that what they were doing was a side interest or a sub-specialty. Embracing humanities computing was not the same as declaring a new theory to be central, redefining a canon, altering institutional constructs, or embracing a new methodology. It was not like distinguishing American History from European History or English Studies from Comparative Literature. Nor was it a purely methodological separation (though, as I have argued, strenuous attempts were made—and continue to be made—to represent the field as bringing the methodologies of science to the humanities). Humanities computing was part of—and, indeed, the result of—the same set of epochal changes that had produced the personal computer and at that very moment were in the process of producing the World Wide Web.

What brought people together from across a startlingly diverse set of disciplines and professional roles was the shift from criticism to creation, from writing to coding, from book to tool. Humanities computing had its theorists, its administrators, its teachers, and its historians, but nearly everyone in the field was involved, in one way or another, with building something.

The conceptual leap required to move from talking about novels to talking about Web sites or computer games requires subtle shifts in thinking and reappraisals of one's assumptions. This remains a vital and fascinating area of investigation for students of new media. But it is nowhere near as jarring—or, frankly, as radical—as the shift from theorizing about games and Web sites to building them. It is true that text encoders often describe working with TEI (Text Encoding Initiative) as an act of interpretation and that builders of software systems have been known to describe their tools as enactments of theories. Yet there remains a world of difference between talking about the different parts of a text and physically separating them with XML tags—between talking about software and writing it. Neither using a map nor considering its status as a cultural representation is to be confused with GIS (geographic information system). The development meeting is not a seminar.

At the same time, people who engage in this kind of building have the clear sense that they have not stopped being humanists or abandoned any of the concerns of the disciplines in which they work and were trained. Most of them came into the field because nothing provided the kind of affordances that are to be found in coding, marking, designing, and building. It is easy enough to describe digital humanities in practical terms as the creation of assistive technologies for use by humanists, but few practitioners would describe their attachment to the field as motivated by utilitarian motives.

Humanists concern themselves with the study of the human experience; digital humanists find that building deepens and enriches that engagement. "Algorithmic criticism" sounds for all the world like a set of methods for exploiting the sudden abundance of digital material related to the humanities. If not a method, then perhaps—and this would be better—a *methodology* for coping with it, handling, it, comprehending it. But in the end, it is simply an attitude toward the relationship between mechanism and meaning that is expansive enough to imagine building as a form of thinking. It resists any approach to computationally assisted literary study that sees the positivistic claims of pure computationalism—the either/or of bare calculation—as the method by which humanistic inquiry may finally, after centuries of insecurity, claim its rightful place as a form of knowledge. At the same time, it rejects the idea that computers, fundamentally incapable of participating fully in the most deeply humane of all scholarly reflections, can only offer "meaningful failure" or object lessons in the limits of computer science. Algorithmic criticism offers a vision of the hacker/scholar as unperturbed by the tension these two words elicit. Its partisans neither worry that criticism is being naively mechanized, nor that algorithms are being pressed beyond their inability. The algorithmic critic imagines the artifacts of human culture as radically transformed, reordered, disassembled, and reassembled. Then he or she, as Father Busa once put it, looks around "for some type of machinery."

NOTES

Chapter 1. An Algorithmic Criticism

1. I am indebted to Sara Steger at the University of Georgia, who was a coinvestigator in the work on computational analysis of Woolf's novel that forms the basis of the following examples. The electronic edition used is from the University of Adelaide Library (http://etext.library.adelaide.edu.au/w/woolf/virginia/w91w).

Chapter 2. Potential Literature

1. All English quotations from *Faustroll* are from Roger Shattuck and Simon Watson Taylor's translation, *Exploits and Opinions of Doctor Faustroll, Pataphysician,* in Jarry, *Selected Works of Alfred Jarry.*

2. The term *Gedankenexperiment* appears in Mach's *The Science of Mechanics: A Critical and Historical Exposition of Its Principles.*

3. Ben Fisher's *The Pataphysician's Library* is a particularly comprehensive study of Jarry's *livres pairs,* which, among other features, participates in the incestuous intertextuality for which Symbolism was particularly famous. As Fisher notes, "It is obvious from an early stage that this novel follows contemporary manners by eulogizing its literary peer group—at length, and in considerable if oblique detail" (4).

4. To which we might add, via Kelvin's *Popular Lectures and Addresses (1855–1887),* the physics of James Clerk Maxwell, Werner von Siemens, Humphry Davy, Rayleigh (John William Strutt, 3rd Baron Rayleigh), Adam Sedgwick, James Dewer, and Michael Faraday, and the mathematics of Claude-Louis Navier, Siméon Denis Poisson, and Augustin-Louis Cauchy. See Stillman's "Physics and Pataphysics: The Sources of *Faustroll.*"

5. See *Oulipo: Atlas de littérature potentielle.*

6. The work in codex form was originally laid out so that each poem was printed on the recto of the leaf and cut into separate strips for each line. The reader could therefore lift up a line to reveal another one beneath.

7. Abish was not a member of Oulipo, though as Harry Mathews and Alastair Brotchie note, "The work must be qualified an Oulipian masterpiece. . . . The method he has used, of his own devising, is Oulipian both in its axiomatic simplicity and in the extent to which it determines both the ingenious narrative and its beguiling linguistic texture" (48).

8. In order for the algorithm to work, the number of rows and columns must be equal. Mathews further notes that a certain amount of heterogeneity is necessary in the data: "The rule is that in a table of *n* elements, *n2 – (n – 2)* elements must be different" (Motte, *Oulipo* 127). The examples that follow are all drawn from "Mathews's Algorithm," in Motte, *Oulipo.*

Chapter 3. Potential Readings

1. Dickinson herself does not precisely define the notion of backwardness in this case, and it may be that we are meant to come at the poem in quite another way:

—blind be man every Or
gradually dazzle must Truth The
kind explanation With
eased Children the to lightning As

surprise superb Truth's The
Delight infirm our for bright Too
lies Circuit in Success
—slant it tell but truth the all Tell

Either procedure can be generated programmatically.

2. The entropic poem is meant to be read column by column.

3. McGann and Samuels go to considerable lengths to demonstrate that the historical antecedents to the notion of deformance are by no means confined to the twentieth-century avant garde. The chapter, in fact, considers deformative procedures "perhaps as ancient as our more normative practices," and draws its chief examples from Dante and Shelley (106).

4. Students and devotees of the *I Ching* will note that my reading of the hexagrams— somewhat after the manner of a tarot card reading—is not consistent with the usual way in which "divination" is understood in the context of this work. Most would say that the ancients regarded the *I Ching* not as a fortune-telling device in the Western sense, but as a book that one consults in order to determine (through poetic means, as it were) the proper strategy for reaching some goal. In the words of the great French explicator of the *I Ching,* "The old Classic of Changes speaks to us because we ask it to. We are the ones who give it this capability" (Javary 116).

5. "sy æt him sylfum gelong; / eal his worulde wyn, / sy ful wide fah / feorres folclondes"

Chapter 4. The Turing Text

1. This standard description differs from the one offered in Turing's 1957 article, "Computing Machinery and Intelligence":

It is played with three people, a man (A), a woman (B), and an interrogator (C) who may be of either sex. The interrogator stands in a room apart from the other two. The object of the game for the interrogator is to determine which of the other two is the man and which is the woman. He knows them by labels X and Y, and at the end of the game he says either "X is A and Y is B" or "X is B and Y is A." (153)

The familiar form of the Turing test comes about when Turing asks a question that he proposes as the equivalent to "Can a machine think?": "What will happen when a machine takes the part of A in this game?"

2. ELIZA (named after the character Eliza Doolittle in Shaw's *Pygmalion*) properly refers to the underlying language-analysis engine that Weizenbaum used to construct DOCTOR. However, the name ELIZA has persisted as a name for the program, and I follow this convention here.

3. See Sigler.

Chapter 5. 'Patacomputing

1. A more detailed discussion of these results, particularly as they relate to authorship attribution, can be found in Hoover's article "Another Perspective on Vocabulary Richness."

WORKS CITED

Aarseth, Espen J. *Cybertext: Perspectives on Ergodic Literature.* Baltimore: Johns Hopkins University Press, 1997.

Abelson, Harold, and Gerald Jay Sussman. *Structure and Interpretation of Computer Programs.* 2nd ed. Cambridge: MIT Press, 1996.

Abish, Walter. *Alphabetical Africa.* New York: New Directions, 1974.

Achebe, Chinua. "An Image of Africa: Racism in Conrad's *Heart of Darkness.*" *Hopes and Impediments: Selected Essays.* New York: Doubleday, 1989. 1–20.

Bayard, Pierre. *How to Talk about Books You Haven't Read.* New York: Bloomsbury USA, 2007.

Bök, Christian. *'Pataphysics: The Poetics of an Imaginary Science.* Evanston, Ill.: Northwestern University Press, 2002.

Bold, Stephen C. "Labyrinths of Invention from the New Novel to OuLiPo." *Neophilologus* 82 (1988): 543–57.

Burrows, J. F., and D. H. Craig. "Lyrical Drama and the 'Turbid Montebanks': Styles of Dialogue in Romantic and Renaissance Tragedy." *Computers and the Humanities* 28 (1994): 63–86.

Busa, Roberto. "The Annals of Humanities Computing: The *Index Thomisticus.*" *Computer and the Humanities* 14 (1980): 83–90.

———. *Index Thomisticus.* Stuttgart: Frommann-Holzboog, 1974.

Bush, Vannevar. "As We May Think." *Atlantic Monthly* July 1945: 101–8. Print.

Buzetti, Dino. "Digital Representation and the Text Model." *New Literary History* 33.1 (2002): 61–88.

Charney, Maurice. *All of Shakespeare.* New York: Columbia University Press, 1993.

Chatbot::ELIZA. Vers. 1.04. 1 March 2008. http://search.cpan.org/CPAN/authors/id/J/ JN/JNOLAN/Chatbot-Eliza-1.04.tar.gz.

Craig, Hugh. "Authorial Attribution and Computational Stylistics: If You Can Tell Authors Apart, Have You Learned Anything about Them?" *Literary and Linguistic Computing* 14 (1999): 103–13.

Deleuze, Gilles, and Félix Guattari. *A Thousand Plateaus: Capitalism and Schizophrenia.* Minneapolis: University of Minnesota Press, 1987.

DeRose, Stephen J., Elli Mylonas, David Durand, and Allen Renear. "What Is Test, Really?" *Journal of Computing in Higher Education* 1 (1990): 3–26.

Derrida, Jacques. "*Ulysses* Gramophone: Hear Say Yes in Joyce." *James Joyce: The Augmented Ninth.* Ed. Bernard Benstock. Syracuse, N.Y.: Syracuse University Press, 1988.

Dickinson, Emily. *Complete Poems of Emily Dickinson.* Ed. Thomas H. Johnson. Boston: Little, Brown, 1960.

Faulkner, William. *Light in August.* New York: Vintage, 1987.

Ferguson, Margaret, Mary Jo Salter, and Jon Stallworthy, eds. *The Norton Anthology of Poetry.* 4th ed. New York: Norton, 1996.

Fisher, Ben. *The Pataphysician's Library: An Exploration of Alfred Jarry's "Livres Pairs."* Liverpool: Liverpool University Press, 2000.

Fortier, Paul A. "Babies, Bathwater and the Study of Literature." *Computers and the Humanities* 27 (1993): 375–85.

Gadamer, Hans-Georg. *Truth and Method.* Trans. Joel Weinsheimer and Donald G. Marshall. New York: Continuum International, 1996.

Garfinkel, Harold. *Studies in Ethnomethodology.* Englewood Cliffs, N.J.: Prentice-Hall, 1967.

Gottschall, Jonathan. "Measure for Measure." *Boston Globe.* 11 May 2008, 3rd ed.: D1.

Haraway, Donna. "A Cyborg Manifesto: Science, Technology, and Socialist-Feminism in the Late Twentieth Century." *Simians, Cyborgs, and Women: The Reinvention of Nature.* New York: Routledge, 1991. 149–81.

Hockey, Susan. *Electronic Texts in the Humanities.* Oxford: Oxford University Press, 2000.

Hoover, David. "Another Perspective on Vocabulary Richness." *Computers and the Humanities* 37.2 (2003): 151–78.

———. "Face of Text." E-mail to Stephen Ramsay. 23 November 2004.

Irizarry, Estelle. "Tampering with the Text to Increase Awareness of Poetry's Art. (Theory and Practice with a Hispanic Perspective)." *Literary and Linguistic Computing* 11 (1996): 155–62.

Jarry, Alfred. *Selected Works of Alfred Jarry.* Eds. Roger Shattuck and Simon Watson Taylor. New York: Grove, 1965.

Javary, Cyrille. *Understanding the I Ching.* Boston: Shambhala, 1997.

Kelvin, William Thomson. *Popular Lectures and Addresses.* Vols. 1–3. London: Macmillan, 1891.

Knuth, Donald. *Fundamental Algorithms.* Vol. 1 of *The Art of Computer Programming.* Reading, Mass.: Addison-Wesley, 1997.

Kuhn, Thomas S. *The Essential Tension: Selected Studies in Scientific Tradition and Change.* Chicago: University of Chicago Press, 1977.

Lear, Edward. *The Complete Nonsense of Edward Lear.* Ed. Holbrook Jackson. Mattituck, N.Y.: Amereon, 1947.

Legge, James, trans. *The Sacred Books of China.* Vol. 2. *Sacred Books of the East* 16. Oxford: Oxford University Press, 1882.

Leslie, R. F. *Three Old English Elegies: The Wife's Lament, The Husband's Message, The Ruin.* New York: Barnes, 1961.

Lewis, Sinclair. Main Street *and* Babbitt. New York: Library of America, 1992.

Lucretius. *On the Nature of Things.* Trans. Martin Ferguson Smith. New York: Hackett, 2001.

Mach, Ernst. *The Science of Mechanics: A Critical and Historical Exposition of Its Principles.* Chicago: Open Court, 1893.

Mandel, Jerome. *Alternative Readings in Old English Poetry.* American University Studies 4.43. New York: Lang, 1987.

Manning, Christopher D., and Hinrich Schütze. *Foundations of Statistical Natural Language Processing.* Cambridge: MIT Press, 1999.

Mathews, Harry, and Alastair Brotchie. *Oulipo Compendium.* London: Atlas, 1998.

McCarty, Willard. *Encyclopedia of Library and Information Science.* Vol. 2. 2nd ed. New York: Dekker, 2003.

McGann, Jerome J., and Lisa Samuels. "Deformance and Interpretation." Chapter 4 of *Radiant Textuality: Literature after the World Wide Web.* New York: Palgrave, 2001.

McLuhan, Marshall. *Understanding Media: The Extensions of Man.* 1964. Cambridge: MIT Press, 1994.

Moretti, Franco. "Conjectures on World Literature." *New Left Review* 1 (2000): 54–68.

———. *Graphs, Maps, Trees: Abstract Models of Literary History.* London: Verso, 2005.

Motte, Warren F., ed. and trans. *Oulipo: A Primer of Potential Literature.* Lincoln: University of Nebraska Press, 1986.

———. "Raymond Queneau and the Aesthetic of Formal Constraint." *Romanic Review* 82.2 (1991): 192–209.

Mueller, Martin. "Digital Shakespeare or Toward a Literary Informatics." *Shakespeare* 4.3 (2008): 284–301.

———. *WordHoard.* Vers. 1.2.8. 29 May 2008. http://wordhoard.northwestern.edu/userman/index.html

Oulipo. *Atlas de littérature potentielle.* Paris: Gallimard, 1981.

Plato. *Plato: The Collected Dialogues.* Ed. Edith Hamilton and Huntington Cairns. Princeton, N.J.: Princeton University Press, 1989.

Pope, Rob. *Textual Intervention: Critical and Creative Strategies for Literary Studies.* London: Routledge, 1995.

Potter, Roseanne G. "Literary Criticism and Literary Computing: The Difficulties of a Synthesis." *Computers and the Humanities* 22 (1988): 91–97.

Queneau, Raymond. *Le Voyage en Grèce.* Paris: Gallimard, 1973.

Ramsay, Stephen. "In Praise of Pattern." *TEXT Technology* 14.2 (2005): 177–90.

Rockwell, Geoffrey. *TAPoR (Text Analysis Portal for Research).* Vers. 1, rev. 1201. 29 May 2008. http://portal.tapor.ca/portal/portal.

———. "TAPoR Portal Recipes." 29 May 2008. Text Analysis Developers Alliance. http://tada.mcmaster.ca/Main/TaporRecipes.

———. "What Is Text Analysis?" 29 May 2008. Text Analysis Developers Alliance. http://tada.mcmaster.ca/Main/WhatTA.

Rockwell, Geoffrey, and Stéfan Sinclair. "There's a Toy in My Essay! Problems with the Rhetoric of Text Analysis." 29 May 2008. GeoffreyRockwell.com. http://www.philosophi.ca/pmwiki.php/Main/TheRhetoricOfTextAnalysis.

Rosenthal, Michael. *Virginia Woolf.* London: Routledge, 1979.

Rutt, Richard, ed. *The Book of Changes (Zhouyi)*. Durham East-Asia Series 1. Richmond, U.K.: Routledge-Curzon Press, 1996.

Schirato, Anthony. "Comic Politics and Politics of the Comic: Walter Abish's Alphabetical Africa." *Critique* 33.2 (1992): 133–34.>

Sedgwick, Eve Kosofsky. *Between Men: English Literature and Male Homosocial Desire*. New York: Columbia University Press, 1985.

Sigler, L. E. *Fibonacci's Liber Abaci: A Translation into Modern English of Leonardo Pisano's Book of Calculation*. New York: Springer, 2002.

Sinclair, Stéfan. *HyperPo*. Vers. 6.0. 29 May 2008. HyperPo: Text Analysis and Exploration Tools. http://tapor.mcmaster.ca/~hyperpo/Versions/6.0.

Snow, Charles Percy. *The Cultures and Scientific Revolution*. Cambridge: Cambridge University Press, 1959.

Starobinsky, Jean. *Words upon Words: The Anagrams of Ferdinand de Saussure*. Trans. Olivia Emmet. New Haven, Conn.: Yale University Press, 1979.

Stillman, Linda Klieger. *Alfred Jarry*. Twayne World Author Series 681. Boston: Twayne, 1983.

———. "Physics and Pataphysics: The Sources of Faustroll." *Kentucky Romance Quarterly* 26 (1979): 81–92.

Suchman, Lucy A. *Plans and Situated Actions: The Problem of Human-Machine Communication*. Cambridge: Cambridge University Press, 1987.

Thomas, Dylan. *The Poems of Dylan Thomas*. New York: New Directions, 2003.

Thomas, Jean-Jacques. "README.DOC: On Oulipo." *Substance* 56 (1988): 18–28.

Turing, A. M. "Computing Machinery and Intelligence." *Mind* 59.236 (1950): 433–60.

Walker-Pelkey, Faye. "'Frige hwæt ic hatte:' 'The Wife's Lament' as Riddle." *Papers on Language and Literature* 28.3 (1992).

Wallace, Miriam L. "Theorizing Relational Subjects: Metonymic Narrative in *The Waves*." *Narrative* 8.3 (2000): 294–323.

Weizenbaum, Joseph. *Computer Power and Human Reason: From Judgment to Calculation*. San Francisco: Freeman, 1976.

Whitehead, Alfred North. *An Introduction to Mathematics*. Oxford: Oxford University Press, 1997.

Wittgenstein, Ludwig. *Philosophical Investigations*. Trans. G. E. M. Anscombe. Oxford: Blackwell, 1992.

———. *Tractatus Logico-Philisophicus*. London: Routledge, 1974.

Woolf, Virginia. "How Should One Read a Book?" *The Second Common Reader: Annotated Edition*. 1932. San Diego: Harvest-HBJ, 1986.

———. *The Waves*. San Diego: Harvest-HBJ, 1931.

Zeitlyn, David. "Divination as Dialogue: Negotiation of Meaning with Random Responses." *Social Intelligence and Interaction: Expressions and Implications of the Social Bias in Human Intelligence*. Ed. Esther N. Goody. Cambridge: Cambridge University Press, 1995.

INDEX

TOPICS IN THE DIGITAL HUMANITIES

From Papyrus to Hypertext: Toward the Universal Digital Library
  *Christian Vandendorpe, translated from the French
  by Phyllis Aronoff and Howard Scott*
Reading Machines: Toward an Algorithmic Criticism   *Stephen Ramsay*

STEPHEN RAMSAY is an associate professor of English at the University of Nebraska and has written and lectured widely on subjects related to literary theory and software design for humanities.

THE UNIVERSITY OF ILLINOIS PRESS is a founding member of the Association of American University Presses.

Title page graphics by Alex DeArmond.

Written using LaTeX (on the command-line of a Linux machine using Vim), edited in Microsoft Word, designed and composed in Adobe InDesign, and reinstantiated with an offset lithographic printing press.

Composed in 10.5/13 Adobe Minion Pro with Trade Gothic display at the University of Illinois Press.
Manufactured by Thomson-Shore, Inc.

University of Illinois Press
1325 South Oak Street
Champaign, IL 61820-6903
www.press.uillinois.edu